"Is your sales pipeline bursting with high quality leads? If not, you *need* this book. It's the best I've ever read on the subject."

—DAVE STEIN, AUTHOR OF *HOW WINNERS SELL*

"Tony Parinello has written a terrific book that answers the toughest questions that today's salesperson must answer—"How do I reach and influence the decision maker?"

—ROGER DAWSON, AUTHOR OF *SECRETS OF POWER NEGIATING*

"Tony is the master of creative selling. I have applied several of his principles personally as well as in my business. Invest in his material—and use it!"

—JAMES ARTHUR RAY, AUTHOR OF *THE SCIENCE OF SUCCESS*

"Oh, what a relief! Tony gives you powerful tools to increase your earnings and practical tips to enhance the fun of it all!"

—GLENNA SALSBURY, AUTHOR OF *THE ART OF THE FRESH START* PROFESSIONAL SPEAKER

"A terrific book that is a must read for any salesperson looking to take their business to the next level. *Stop Cold Calling Forever* is about so much more than how to prospect. It teaches you how—through a fundamental sales process and understanding of today's market—to turn true opportunities into closed deals. It's about opening doors, not closing sales. Guaranteed to make you money. *The Selling to Vito* master has done it again!"

—TODD NATENBERG, AUTHOR OF "I JUST GOT A JOB IN SALES! NOW WHAT?" *A PLAYBOOK FOR SKYROCKETING YOUR COMMISSIONS*, AND PRESIDENT OF TBN SALES SOLUTIONS

"What every salesperson seeks is a knowledgeable, challenging, and very smart coach. Look no further! Tony Parinello does it all in his new book, *Stop Cold Calling Forever*. Follow his excellent advice and enjoy his clever style and you will become the outstanding salesperson you deserve to be."

—DOROTHY LEEDS, THE QUESTIONING CRUSADER AND AUTHOR OF *THE 7 POWERS OF QUE*

"Tony's latest book captures the essence of how to sell in today's marketplace. It is accurate, practical, real-world and tells you step-by-step exactly how to be a sales champion. Get this book! Better yet, read and use it!"

—BILL BROOKS, AUTHOR, *THE NEW SCIENCE OF SELLING AND PERSUASION*

"Tony Parinello has done it again! If you think *Selling to VITO* was a runaway best seller wait until you read *Stop Cold Calling Forever*. It addresses an even bigger problem for a bigger number of salespeople—Cold Calling. What I like best about Parinello's books—they're simple to read and loaded with practical ideas that can be successfully applied immediately. This book is a winner!"

—DR. TONY ALESSANDRA, AUTHOR OF *NON-MANIPULATIVE SELLING AND THE PLATINUM RULE*

"For decades we've insisted that modern sales professionals should be able to 1) comfortably make cold calls when they are necessary, and 2) be trained so completely and effectively they're never necessary. But until now, few legitimate sales authorities have brought useable focus and clarity to the second part of our assertion. Tony Parinello, who introduced the sales profession to VITO, has fixed that oversight. *Stop Cold Calling Forever!* features Parinello's signature, level-headed realism—and unmistakable love for the sales profession. The step-by-step procedures he provides are radically complete. Pages are not wasted on fluff or endless "war stories." Here, salespeople will find the help they need to renovate their sales competencies to the point where cold calling becomes obsolete and irrelevant."

—GEORGE W. DUDLEY & SHANNON L. GOODSON, AUTHORS OF *THE PSYCHOLOGY OF SALES CALL RELUCTANCE*

"Who likes to do cold calling? Not me, and my guess is most of the millions of salespeople in America don't either. It's something we do because "we have to." I'm amazed how uniquely and effectively Tony turns this unpleasant and often frightening activity into a joyful challenge. This book leaves nothing out to help you be a success at cold calling while learning valuable, reliable, and creative sales ideas and methods that will increase your sales. His rational and engaging step-by-step approach makes it easy for anyone to successfully apply Tony's methods to their own specific selling situation. Tony, you did it again— what an ingenious work of art!"

—MADELYN BURLEY-ALLEN, AUTHOR OF *DYNAMICS OF HUMAN BEHAVIOR*

"Anthony Parinello shows salespeople how to conquer one of their biggest fears, cold calling. Tony's book coaches you on how to research prospects so they welcome your initial contact. Each chapter provides you with powerful tools and real-life examples to turn theory into practical applications that are custom-tailor to your selling situations. After you finish this book, you realize that the old ways to do cold calling was just another way to say you didn't do your homework. Tony obviously did his."

—JOSH COSTELL, AUTHOR OF *THE SCIENCE OF SALES SUCCESS*

"Once again, Tony has brought his unique insights into selling in a timely book that offers creative alternatives to the cold call—and the strategies to perform them. Whether the reader is the level entry salesperson or the seasoned professional, he/she will learn from Tony's extraordinary ability to teach."

—ANN DEVINE, CEO, PI SIGMA EPSILON, INC., NATIONAL PROFESSIONAL FRATERNITY IN SALES MANAGEMENT, SELLING, AND MARKETING

STOP COLD CALLING FOREVER!

TRUE CONFESSIONS OF A REFORMED SERIAL COLD-CALLER

ANTHONY PARINELLO

EP
Entrepreneur.
Press

Managing editor: Jere L. Calmes
Cover design: Beth Hansen-Winter
Composition and production: Eliot House Productions

This publication is designed to provide accurate and authoritative information in regard to the subject matter covered. It is sold with the understanding that the publisher is not engaged in rendering legal, accounting, or other professional services. If legal advice or other expert assistance is required, the services of a competent professional person should be sought.

Library of Congress Cataloging-in-Publication Data

Parinello, Anthony.
   Stop cold calling forever!: true confessions of a reformed serial cold caller/Anthony Parinello.
     p.   cm.
   Includes index.
   ISBN 1-932531-16-5
   1. Telephone selling. 2. Telemarketing. I. Title
HF5438.3.P37 2004
658.8'5—dc22   2004056278

Printed in Canada

10 09 08 07 06 05   10 9 8 7 6 5 4 3 2 1

Contents

PART I

Laying the Foundation

CHAPTER ONE

Who's Who?

CHAPTER TWO

Breaking It Down

PART II

Getting Your Message Across

Acknowledgments

THANKS TO ALL OF MY SUPPORTERS AT ENTREPRENEUR PRESS: PETER SHEA, Neil Perlman, Lynea Askey, Jere Calmes, Leanne Harvey, and Shannon Grillo.

And to my editor Karen Billipp for her hard work and beautiful layout. Thanks to my team at Parinello Inc.: Yvonne Davis, Miki Davis, and Beth Allen for keeping the office running during this project. Thanks to Kathleen Brooks and Steve Dailey for their contributions. A special thanks to my many customers and alumni who keep me on my toes always stretching beyond my comfort zone.

And here's to you my new friend, you, for reading and learning from this book. I look forward to getting to know you.

Foreword

THE FIRST DAY I SAW ANTHONY FRANK PARINELLO HE WAS ON TRIAL FOR being a compulsive, habitual, serial cold caller. A menace to the business society.

The judge's words were cutting and hard. "Anthony," he said, "you represent the bottom of the business food chain. I get sick thinking of the billions of dollars that are wasted in our economy by the likes of you." He shifted in his chair and leaned forward to make more direct eye contact with Tony.

"You and your compatriots in this cult you call cold-call selling are, frankly, a disgrace to the profession of selling," he bellowed. "The lack of planning, the lack of productivity, and the willingness to waste good people's time—you should be ashamed of yourself! My better judgment says I should put you away for life. Extracting you from the marketplace is, in my opinion, the only sensible justice. But a second thought causes me to seek a remedy for *all* of society instead, and put an end to this madness once and for all. You need to be an example. You can serve as a remedy to the problem."

He stared long and hard at Tony.

"I'm going to sentence you to one year of isolation. During that time you're to create a sales training program that will stop cold calling forever, Mr. Parinello." He paused, and then beckoned to me. I stepped forward.

"After you complete your sentence and the creation of your program, I instruct you to report to Parole Officer Steve Dailey for a period of one year. He will become your coach in declaring war on our business society's greatest menace—cold calling."

One Year Later

Inmate E8486, Anthony Frank Parinello, emerged from confinement. As Tony's eyes met mine, I noticed a sparkle. "Mr. Dailey," he whispered, "I have the answer for all of the cold-calling junkies in our selling culture today!" He waved his journal, inches from my nose. "It's in here," he said. "It's all in here! My true confessions!"

We turned to walk inside the diner where we had agreed to meet on the day of his release. Over several cups of coffee and a couple of burgers, Tony went through the realizations, flashes of insight, and personal discoveries that had rained down upon him during his lonely sentence. He went page by page in his journal, recounting strategies, principles, and directives that, as we continued to speak, not only made sense but began to ring true as potentially a new beginning for sales professionals across the nation.

When he finally paused to get my reaction, I simply said these words: "Tony, you're on to something big, really big. Now you need to prove it."

At that, he leapt from his seat, shaking my hand vigorously. He assured me that I would not regret giving him a chance to save the profession of sales. His eyes were bouncing and his smile lit up the whole joint. He grabbed me by the shoulder and led me out of the door, sharing more and more details about his system, his strategy, his game plan to *Stop Cold-Calling Forever!*

The book you are holding culminates the work of a man who has paid his debt to society.

Don't treat this lightly. Don't make the same mistake Tony did. Learn from the book you hold in your hands.

One Sentence of Advice

Don't just read this book. *USE* it as though your sales career depended upon it. Because it does!

—Steve Dailey

To
Alexander Graham Bell
One of My Heroes

Laying the Foundation

I HOPE YOU DECIDED TO READ THIS BOOK FOR ONE OF TWO REASONS:

1. You are sick and tired of making cold calls, and you've decided that you're not going to take it anymore.

2. You love making cold calls, but you have a feeling, deep down inside, that they are not part of the task of learning how to sell more successfully in this economy.

Either premise works as a point of entry for this book.

Beyond the Cold Call

Whether you're a veteran salesperson, a newcomer to the game, or a sales manager/sales leader looking for new ideas for his or her team, you want answers to these questions:

- Do I really have to make cold calls?
- How can I make my sales work more effective?
- How can I attract more new customers without getting rejected, oh, let's say, 150 times a day?
- How can I hold on to and grow the customer base that I already have?

I've met over 1 million salespeople eyeball to eyeball, and they ask me similar questions. The good news is that you really can work more effectively, attract more new customers, and grow your customer base—without making cold calls. This book shows you how.

The way I see it, the work of a professional salesperson includes:

- Prospecting for new business
- Probing for needs
- Creating proposals
- Making presentations
- Answering objections
- Negotiating
- Asking for the business

Time is at a premium. And competition is brutal. So it's incumbent upon salespeople to learn how to carry out these tasks *more effectively than in years past—and more effectively than the competition is doing right now.*

Guess what? Making cold calls is not part of that equation!

No Shortcuts

There are no shortcuts here. Selling is, and always has been, hard work. This book is designed to make your selling routine more efficient ... but I'm afraid that's not the same thing as making selling easy!

So get started. It's time to do some pick-and-shovel work. I've put the biggest task upfront, in the early part of the book, so you can get it out of the way. Once it's done, I promise you won't have to do it again—and *you'll be one step closer to a cold-call-free model of selling.*

Ready? Let's go.

NO COLD-CALLING PRINCIPLE 1

"The only good prospect is
one who is predisposed
to buy from you."

—E8486

Who's Who?

THE CRITICAL FIRST STEP IN THE COLD-CALL-FREE SELLING MODEL IS DEFIN-
ING what organizations would be predisposed to buy from you. A sub-
step of this step is identifying the key individual(s) within these
organizations.

The operative words here are *predisposed* and *individual(s)*. In this
chapter you'll discover a way to prequalify the organizations (yes, you read
right, *prequalify*), and you'll create a target list of prequalified, predisposed
organizations. In Chapter Two the focus is on the individuals within those
organizations.

Listen up. If you don't carry out the tasks outlined in these first two chapters, you are essentially declining the invitation to work in a cold-call-free
selling environment.

It's up to you. If you decide to keep reading—and I hope you will—
please complete all the assignments I give you. OK? And you'll be invited

to go online and get additional information and do additional exercises. That's right, I've created a special Learning Center for your continual self-improvement in what will become your cold-call-free world.

To Buy or Not to Buy

It never ceases to amaze me how many salespeople act as if their job description includes "beat a dead horse." They spend sales call after sales call, voice-mail message after voice-mail message, and presentation after presentation trying to persuade their prospect to buy from them. What a waste of time.

> Do not fall into the trap of mistaking activity for results. There really is a way to target, visit, and sell to only those organizations and individuals who are truly predisposed to buy from you. To pull this off, you have to . . .

Get Your Head Straight

Focus on learning everything you possibly can about your territory as a whole. Take all those old complaints you've heard other salespeople make about their territories—"There aren't enough companies," "It's been split too many times," "The last rep who had my territory didn't make her/his quota," "It's not the right demographics for our product"—and drag them all into a folder, click on the folder, and deposit the whole mess into the Recycle Bin. Now activate the Recycle Bin and hit "Empty."

You are now out of excuses and formally in charge of your territory and every enterprise that resides within it. You, and you alone, are in control of your own career.

Doesn't that feel better?

Forget about Routines

You may have an established routine when it comes to connecting with people who may buy from you. I'm going to ask you to trash that routine, too, and take full advantage of a powerful sales tool: the Template of Ideal Prospects, or TIP sheet.

> True sales excellence involves thinking in the long term, act-
> ing in the short term, and developing the capacity to highlight
> creative solutions. Start thinking about yourself as less of a
> sales rep and more of a trusted advisor or thought partner.

The TIP sheet is the list of characteristics shared by your company's best customers.

"Wait a minute, Tony. I don't have any customers. Remember, it's the beginning of a new year." "I am a hunter." "I just started this job." "I just got a new territory."

Worry not. Remember, the focus is on your company's best customers. Just about every company has a customer or two you can model this process on. My promise to you is that if you take this step and live by this presales call process, you'll never, ever again waste your time calling on a company that won't buy from you. And you'll never have to make another cold call!

On the Road Again

Grab your company's current customer list, a notebook, or perhaps a small personal tape recorder. You'll also need a pen or pencil and a large pad of paper! Put aside your laptop, palmtop, PDA, and/or cell phone. You'll have no need for these timesavers.

Head for the Door

No, you're not going out to make a sales call or take a friend to lunch. You're bound for the library—the one in your area with a business research department worthy of the name.

Maybe you're thinking: "Tony, what's wrong with the Internet?"

Everything is wrong with the Internet. For starters, your competition is looking at the Internet. Let's just stop there, shall we? Trust me, the library is where you need to be.

Once you're at the library, take a good, long look at that customer list you brought along. Then ask yourself the following question:

What do my company's best current customers have in common?

A Momentous Question

Success leaves clues, a little trail of breadcrumbs that when retraced will take you back to success—and so do your best customers. You'll be using all the library resources at your disposal to find answers to the key questions about your organization's existing customer base, by working your way through the Template of Ideal Prospects sheet you'll find later in this chapter.

The customer list you'll be reviewing may need to be broken down into subgroups. If you're selling a product, service, or solution that's of interest to both life sciences organizations and the entertainment industry, you'll find that the specifics of each group should be taken into account. You'll also notice that different subgroups may have some limited number of commonalities—more breadcrumbs. You'll be filling out a different TIP sheet for each of the industries, subgroups, or niches to which you want to sell.

Look at that first question once again: "What do my company's best current customers have in common?" You may be tempted to answer by saying, "Hey, I know 'em when I see 'em," or some variation. Don't fall into that trap.

Get specific. You owe your quota-busting, no cold-calling career the fullest possible answer.

Take a look at the blank TIP sheet that follows. Make several copies for your own use, or visit www.stopcoldcalling.info for copies you can print out. If you take the time to use the library's resources to develop detailed, meaningful first-draft answers to each of the sections of the TIP sheet, and if you then transfer your work onto a duplicate of this form for a second draft, you will be well on your way to finding every potential customer in your sales territory—and putting an end to cold-calling as we know it.

Read the three questions on this TIP sheet carefully before you proceed any further.

Taken together, all of this information will provide you with a reliable portrait of your ideal customer—and yes, your ideal prospects, too. This portrait will also help you quickly locate your best new-customer opportunities, save you lots of time, and prevent you from confusing sales activity with sales results. And perhaps more important, when combined with what you'll be learning in the rest of this book, it will save you from ever making a cold call again.

FIGURE 1.1: TIP Sheet

Template of Ideal Prospects   Industry:_____ Category: _____
Fill in all information completely.

What are the titles of the:
- Approver   _____
- Decision Maker(s)   _____
- Influencer(s)   _____
- Recommender(s)   _____

List three problems you can solve by category:

Category   Problem
- Approver   _____
                    _____
                    _____

- Decision Maker(s) _____
                    _____
                    _____

- Influencer(s)   _____
                    _____
                    _____

- Recommender(s)   _____
                    _____
                    _____

My best customers in this industry have:
- between   _____and   _____ [salespeople]
- between   _____ and   _____ [sales regions]
- between   _____ and   _____ [annual revenue]
- between   _____ and   _____ [customers]
- between   _____ and   _____ [suppliers]
- between   _____ and   _____ [other parameter]

Other unique identifiers:

_____
_____
_____
_____

The Ultimate Timesaver: It's Your First Step

Even if you hate research, are a better doer than planner, and don't have time for paperwork, *spending at least a full eight-hour day in the library to develop your TIP sheet(s) will be a great investment in your career.*

The TIP sheet will also help you create attention-getting written material and opening statements, which will, as you will soon see, play a very important role in your cold-call-free selling model.

As if all that weren't enough, the TIP sheet will allow you to develop other tools you can use to get the attention of key decision makers who are predisposed to buy from you.

What It Looks Like When Complete

Here is an example of a TIP sheet that has been completely filled out. Read it for reference and to get an idea of the kind of information you'll be tracking down during that full day (minimum!) in the library. Don't assume that the answers that appear on the sample TIP sheet below will have anything whatsoever to do with the answers that apply to your territory or your business. What you're about to read is my personal TIP.

Let's say that's your best customer. In evaluating any new prospect, you would compare its characteristics to those on that list. *The more matches there are, the more predisposition the prospect will have to buy from you.*

Sell

If you're not experiencing a burning desire to go to the library now, you should be. It's part of the first step in your new cold-call-free SELLing model. The key word here is, of course, *SELL*:

Select…Engage…Launch…Listen

Once you've completed your first eight hours (minimum) of research at the library, it will be time to—head back to the library.

Oh, stop groaning. I told you there was some pick-and-shovel work here. Buckle down, and get it over with. Which is more painful, a couple of evenings at the library or a couple of years' worth of cold calls?

FIGURE 1.2: Completed TIP Sheet

Template of Ideal Prospects   Industry:_____ Category: _____
Fill in all information completely.

What are the titles of the:

- Approver _____President_____
- Decision Maker(s) ___V.P. sales_____
- Influencer(s) ___Sales trainer, Area sales manager_____
- Recommender(s) ___Sales manager_____

List three problems you can solve by category:

Category	Problem
· Approver	1. Compression of time to market.
	2. Getting add-on business from existing customers.
	3. Cutting nonvalue expense.
· Decision Maker(s)	1. Consistency in sales forecasting.
	2. Increase face-to-face selling time.
	3. Greater motivation of entire sales team.
· Influencer(s)	1. Cutting-edge intellectual work.
	2. Well-known specialist "on staff."
	3. Plugs and plays with current sales process.
· Recommender(s)	1. Eliminate cold calls and rejection.
	2. Close more sales faster.
	3. Make every sale a bigger sale.

My best customers in this industry have:

- between _____100_____and _____500_____ [salespeople]
- between _____3_____ and _____5_____ [sales regions]
- between ___$50,000___ and _$500,000,000_ [annual revenue]
- between _____ and _____ [customers]
- between _____ and _____ [suppliers]
- between _____ and _____ [other parameter]

Other unique identifiers:

_Involved in a "complex sale."_____
_Invest in sales training on a regular basis._____
_Hire outside consultants._____
_Have yearly sales kickoff meetings._____

11

Four Big Ideas

1. Read and understand the questions on the TIP sheet.

2. Hit the library (tomorrow morning) and develop the fullest possible answers to the questions on the TIP sheet. It will take at least eight hours.

3. Identify all the names of all the organizations in your territory that match your TIP sheet. It may take you another eight hours.

4. Stop whining about how much library time you're investing. It will all be worth it.

Bonus Idea

While you're at the library, take the time to check out a self-help, self-development book, and read it.

Don't forget to go to: www.stopcoldcalling.info for additional for-fee information on this chapter. Click on "Chapter One: Online Assets."

Notes

NO COLD-CALLING
PRINCIPLE 2

"Always know the answer

to the question:

Who's who?"

—E8486

Breaking It Down

NOW YOU KNOW WHICH ORGANIZATIONS ARE MOST LIKELY TO BE PREDISPOSED to buying whatever it is you happen to be selling. In order to change your selling model, you'll need to take two more steps:

1. Divide each of these organizations into one of three categories.
2. Select the right person to engage with.

In this chapter, you'll complete Item 1, and you'll also learn the categories that will allow you to start working on Item 2.

Three Categories

What is your territory? It could be:

- a geographic area
- a named and somewhat protected list of accounts
- a niche of any number of industry-specific organizations

- a subset of somebody else's territory
- even the entire world!

No matter how you slice the territory up, what you call it, or what resides in your sales territory, you will find that it consists of one, two, or all three of the following categories:

1. *Suspects.* Companies or individuals who are potential customers, but who have *not yet* had any direct contact with you or your organization.
2. *Prospects.* These are people whom you *have contacted,* or who have contacted you, and who fit the TIP that we created in Chapter One. In other words, they represent a realistic potential for future business.
3. *Customers.* These are the folks who have made a decision to purchase what you have to offer and are *currently buying* from you. The operative word here is *currently.* If someone has your product, service, or solution but is not currently buying from you, by default you are looking at a prospect—someone who by definition fits your TIP sheet to a T.

Note that any one of the above categories may be a great source for referrals. (The important topic of referrals is covered in detail later in the book.)

Update Your Target List

Now take all of the TIP sheets that you created in Chapter One. In the blank spot, enter the appropriate category—Suspect, prospect, or customer. Then separate all of your TIP sheets into three piles. Take a long, careful look at the three stacks of paper.

By the way, if you've been reading along passively and skipped the pick-and-shovel steps where you were supposed to do the research at the library, you now have no stacks of paper to look at. You have confirmed only that you are wasting both your reading time and the money you spent on this book. At this point, you have two choices: Put the book aside and start reading again when you're willing to make an investment in your own career, or toss the book into the garbage and bury the purchase price in your expenses as a cheap customer lunch.

Assuming you really do have three stacks of paper in front of you, guess what? What's in front of you is your bread and butter. What's in front of you will drive your prospecting activities and feed your sales process. What's in front of you will generate performance levels beyond your wildest imagination.

Now the question becomes: With whom in these three categories of accounts will you engage?

Four Roles

No matter what category of organization you base your sales efforts on—suspect, prospect, or customer—you will have four basic roles, or areas of responsibility, waiting in the cold-call-free selling model.

No matter what you're selling or to whom you're selling, you will inevitably find that your audience consists of these four important roles. So let's identify with whom you're dealing.

1. *Role One.* This is an individual or a group of individuals who will recommend your products, services, and solutions to their organization and higher-ups. I call the person or persons playing this role the *Recommender(s)*.

2. *Role Two.* This is an individual or group of individuals who will influence the decision to purchase your products, services, and solutions by the higher-ups. I call the person or persons playing this role the *Influencer(s)*.

3. *Role Three.* This is an individual who will actually make the decision to purchase your products, services, and solutions. I call the person playing this role the *Decision Maker*.

4. *Role Four.* This is an individual who will actually approve the decision and money to purchase your products, services, and solutions. I call the person playing this role the *Approver*.

That's it. That's the whole cast of characters. Everyone you meet will fall into one of these four slots. Notice that Roles One and Two can be played by more than one person, even by a committee. However, the roles of the Decision Maker and Approver are most often played solo—and could even be played by the same person.

The presence of people in any one or more of these roles may not always be immediately apparent to you. Let's look closely at all four categories, and make sure you totally understand each role.

The Recommender

Have you ever been asked to serve as a member of a committee that was given the task to brainstorm some new ideas on how to do something faster, easier, or more accurately? Were you even asked to consider eliminating something altogether? If you answered "yes" to any of these questions, congratulations. You've had the privilege of being asked to play the role of Recommender.

In each organization you try to sell to, there are large groups of people who spend their days actually doing what other people plan, outline, set up, and evaluate. These folks—whether they be receptionists, assistants, editors, analysts, or contributors in any other category—may well be invited to play the role of the Recommender, and thus can have an impact on your efforts to land the sale.

Recommenders can be found just about anywhere in an organization, from the janitor's room to the boardroom. Education level, gender, talent, or intelligence quotient may not matter much—anyone and everyone can be a Recommender. What *does* matter is this: Recommenders make recommendations (often based on direct experience) that can carry an awful lot of weight.

Notice that I said the recommendations offered *can* carry an awful lot of weight. But they don't *always* carry a lot of weight. Any recommendation is like an opinion. It may be followed—or it may be ignored.

The Influencer

Influencers live to be right. They are, not infrequently, technical experts who love to win arguments and prove that all the facts are exactly as they've described them. Influencers get a special pleasure out of arguing their position successfully. They get a charge out of the praise and recognition that comes from correctly identifying the problem and the solution, and see their own status as rooted in that praise and recognition. If they were canines in a competition, Influencers would be the ones who considered themselves best in breed.

As a rule, Influencers tend to be fairly critical about any new initiative. Think scientist or engineer—these are the folks who look to *disprove* all competing ideas, remove them by the process of elimination, and in so doing prove their own point. (They often deny that this is how they operate, and offer arguments to *disprove* the contentions of people who say they live to disprove what other people are saying.)

Influencers also make a habit of guarding their information and criteria. Unlike Recommenders, they'll make you connect all the dots yourself. They play things very close to the vest. They know all the rules other people don't, and they know how to follow them to their advantage.

The Decision Maker

In today's business world, the Decision Maker is the person who can *endorse* something the Recommender or Influencer signs off on—someone empowered to make a yes decision about implementing the solution.

Once the Decision Maker makes a yes decision, he or she passes the matter along to the approver for the approval. When we get a no answer from the Decision Maker, that only means someone else (like our competition) has gotten the yes answer.

It's important to understand that the *job of the Decision Maker is to say yes to somebody.* Contrary to popular belief, these people do not have veto power for the opportunity and/or corporate strategic initiative. That ultimate veto power belongs to the Approver.

The Approver

The Approver sits at the top of the corporate totem pole.

These are the individuals whom I respectfully refer to as VITOs: Very Important Top Officers. I wrote about them at length in my first book on sales, *Selling to VITO.*™ These VITOs—who may have titles like Chief

> Whatever you choose to call this person, keep in mind that the Approver has *no limits, no budget, and no one to get approval from.* Power, control, and authority are critically important to these folks, and because of that they tend to be very fast on their feet and very decisive. Now as a general rule, they will support any ideas or strategic corporate initiatives that, when accomplished, will assist them in the *overachievement of their vision.*

Executive Officer, Owner, Senator, Chief of Police, or some other variation on Top Banana—have the ultimate *veto* power. That makes them the ultimate Approver.

These Approvers will pick the appropriate person on their team of Decision Makers (whatever their actual title) and empower that person to look at all the tactical ways to make the vision a reality—by a certain deadline.

The marching orders might sound something like this: *"I need greater control and visibility. Find me the best accounting system in the world that will do the job and fit the budget I've given you."*

So it is that the Decision Maker of choice (maybe the Chief Financial Officer) appoints an Influencer to select a Recommender (say, a head accountant) or assemble a group of Recommenders (such as representatives from the credit department, accounting, order entry, customer service, or collections). These folks are then instructed to: "Find every single accounting package in the world that exceeds our needs and is under budget."

If you have an eagle eye, you just picked up on the addition of two key phrases to the initiative: *exceeds our needs* (rather than "best accounting system in the world") and *under budget* (rather than "fit the budget"). The additions are concepts that Decision Makers are likely to throw into the equation—not Approvers.

Knowledge Really Is Power

OK, you're one step closer to being ready to engage with the suspects, prospects, and customers in your sales territory.

I say "almost ready" because you must first assemble your knowledge about your company and your products in a way that will help you communicate it effectively to the Recommenders, Influencers, Decision Makers, and Approvers you talk to.

You read right: From this point forward in your sales career, you will never, ever deliver the same message to individuals in different roles. Each of these very different players will be engaged using totally different messaging philosophies, because what works with one of them will fail spectacularly with another.

Eight Big Ideas

1. Identify your suspects.

2. Identify your prospects.

3. Identify your customers.

4. Understand the Recommender role.

5. Understand the Influencer role.

6. Understand the Decision Maker role.

7. Understand the Approver role.

8. Get real! If you're not going to do the territory research that allows you to put these distinctions to work, throw this book away or put it aside until you're serious about actually using it.

Notes

NO COLD-CALLING PRINCIPLE 3

"Never use the
same message with
a different audience."

—E8486

CHAPTER THREE

Different Strokes for Different Folks

A LWAYS REMEMBER, WHAT'S HOT TO A RECOMMENDER IS NOT GOING TO BE hot to a Decision Maker or Approver.

What will break through the current preoccupation of an Influencer's day may not make any sense whatsoever to an Approver.

Assuming Responsibility

As a sales professional, your awareness of and responsibility for what your company does must cross all departmental lines. And you must take responsibility, too, for translating your knowledge appropriately to other people.

Here's a preview of coming attractions that will show up a little later in this book. File it away for now. Don't try to memorize it. Just understand that when you get to the point that you're targeting your message to

> You have to craft your messages intelligently to members of each group. In this chapter, you'll learn how to do just that.

specific people within the target organization, this is the sort of system you're going to have to use.

- *Approvers* typically want to buy whatever will help them over-achieve their goals at any price.
- *Decision Makers* usually want to get the job done ahead of schedule and under budget.
- *Influencers* will want the latest and greatest stuff, with NO risk.
- *Recommenders* typically want anything that will make their job easier.

As I say, you'll be learning a lot more about the objectives of each of these four groups a little later on in the book. For now, just understand that you must commit to finding out, discussing intelligently, and interpreting anything and everything that relates to these people. That means you're responsible for discussing—and translating—*just about everything in your organization.*

Why do you have to do this? Because to your suspects, prospects, and customers, you are the company. That means you should be able to communicate effectively about it.

You are the first (and sometimes the only) contact your suspects, prospects, and customers will have with your organization. It is your responsibility to talk to and, if necessary, meet with all the various departments within your organization. It is your responsibility to understand what it is that your company does that no competitor could possibly do. And it is your responsibility to convey that message in a dramatic and comprehensible way based on the role of the person you're talking to.

If you sell widgets, get out and visit your manufacturing facility, repair facility, and shipping and customer-care centers. If you resell parts manufactured elsewhere, consider finding some way (physically or virtually) to go to that facility and take a look at the processes that are critical to making your product what it is. If your company offers some kind of service, take a trip out to the front lines and take a look at what your customer is receiving.

At this point, somebody usually interrupts me and says,

"Yeah, but I'm a salesperson, not a tech person, I don't even understand half of this stuff!"

Then steal a tech person.

During the years when I sold computers for Hewlett-Packard, I took many a prospect and many a customer on HP factory tours. Showing off our facilities was a pleasant experience because, frankly, they were pretty impressive operations. This was (and, I'm sure, still is) topnotch, totally high-tech, cutting-edge stuff, complete with all the sci-fi movie visuals: passage through clean rooms that required white smocks, hats, and gloves; acres of blinking lights; and long rows of beeping machines.

On one such tour, my customer expressed amazement at the amount of sophisticated automated manufacturing and test equipment that was used to measure and control the Hewlett-Packard manufacturing process. Once this equipment was pointed out to me, I had to admit that I was amazed, too.

I did a little digging after the tour and found out that every single piece of equipment being used on the Hewlett-Packard line was manufactured by guess who? Hewlett-Packard.

I knew that HP had gotten its start in the test and measurement world, but before that day I had no idea that we made all the stuff necessary to control an entire manufacturing plant from start to finish.

In the weeks that followed, I decided to act on a hunch: I began to get the test equipment salesperson in my office involved in my most important new sales opportunities. Guess what? He added value to my sale, and he was able to look into different areas of the prospect's company, areas I was not aware of and would probably never have asked about.

When Money Talks—Listen!

Sure, I could have simply kept on selling computer systems, and let the test and measurement guys keep to themselves. But I didn't. I found out a little more about a new (to me) area of my company, and I figured out how it might help me in the job of relaying the new information to my customers.

What happened? My sales started to get bigger. Each and every sale I made where I introduced my test equipment counterpart resulted in above-average initial orders. By knowing exactly, not approximately, what my company did, I was able to increase the size of my entry-point orders. From then on in my sales career, I made sure to keep my eyes open for any new advantage my company could offer my prospects and customers, and for any initiative, in any area, that affected my daily sales routine. You should, too.

Added Value

Since my tenure at HP, I've worked for many different organizations. One thing has been consistent, though: my customers always seem to figure out how to use my products, services, and solutions in ways that my marketing and product development folks never knew existed. One of my goals in life is to spot added value that marketing people miss.

Remember, added value is exactly what people buy. It's what separates you from the competition. Make no mistake. With each year that passes, technology brings the competition closer and closer to your offerings. *The only real differences are you and the added value you uncover and then deliver for each unique setting.*

Seven Big Ideas

1. What's "hot" to one person in your target company may be inconsequential, or incomprehensible, to another.

2. Approvers typically want _____.

3. Decision Makers usually want _____.

4. Recommenders will want _____.

5. Influencers typically want _____.

6. When in doubt, steal a tech person.

7. The difference between you and your competition is the unique added value you identify and deliver.

Notes

NO COLD-CALLING PRINCIPLE 4

"Value is in the eye
of the prospect.
The only way to see it
is their way!"

—E8486

CHAPTER FOUR

Crossroads

W E'VE REACHED AN IMPORTANT PART OF THIS BOOK.

If there's one thing I've learned over the years as a salesperson, sales trainer, and radio and Internet talk-show host, it's that salespeople must sell themselves first.

Once a prospect buys you, you can then sell your products, services, and solutions—but not one second before.

The purpose of this book, as you've no doubt gathered by now, is to begin that process of "buying" painlessly and without cold calling. There is a process that will allow you to establish yourself as a valuable part of the sales transaction. One of the critical first steps in that process is what I call a *Personal Value Inventory*.

It represents something of a crossroads for you because it takes a bit of soul-searching to create. And that's not all. Once you've completed that step, you must then go on to create a Product/Service Value Inventory, which also takes a little work.

So this is another decision point for you in terms of this book. Are you going to carry out the program, or are you going to find reasons not to? Good, let's continue.

My promise to you is that if you concentrate on these two critical steps and give them your undivided attention, you'll emerge as a feared competitor, set yourself far apart from the competition, and find it incredibly easy to establish a kind of brand awareness of yourself and your stuff before you ever connect with your contact by phone.

But to do that, you have to know precisely where you add value.

Personal Value

When I ask people to tell me what specifically sets them apart from their competition, I typically get a long silence and a "deer in the headlights" look in return. That's not the answer I want you to give.

Take the time right now to complete the exercise that follows, and you'll have the answer that will set you apart from your closest competitor.

Get a big piece of paper, and copy the basic form you see on the next page, which I call a Personal Value Inventory. First, write your entire name on the top of the form (no initials allowed). If you're married and female, please go the extra distance and add your maiden name.

Now you're going to use your name as an acronym! For each letter in your name, select a word that you feel accurately describes your values, qualities, personality traits, and habits—at least most of the time.

- *Rule Number 1.* You aren't your stuff. Stay away from words that would describe a favorite hobby, your career, or material possessions.
- *Rule Number 2.* Do this on your own. Take your time with this exercise. If you get stuck, as a last resort use a dictionary or thesaurus. Under no circumstances should you have anyone help you develop the words you associate with yourself. The point at this stage is to develop *your own memorable list of words to match the letters in your name.*

Take a look at my name as an acronym.

<u>A N T H O N Y F R A N K P A R I N E L L O</u>

Values and Beliefs	Qualities and Traits
Trustworthy	Aggressive
Honest	Nurturing
Forthright	Overgenerous
Loyal	Reliable
Esteemed	Nimble
Affectionate	Yes (I live by the word "yes")
Noble	Nonconforming
Purposeful	Reckless
Altruistic	Knowledgeable
	Intuitive
	Lighthearted
	Optimistic

That's me. And here's the point: Once I settle on the words, it's impossible for me to forget them.

Values and Beliefs

Values and beliefs are core operating principles. If you compromise or deviate in the smallest way from your values and beliefs, you can usually count on short- or long-term negative consequences, perhaps even severe ones.

Qualities and Traits

People may not always display qualities and traits under every circumstance. For instance, having a good sense of humor can be considered a quality or trait, rather than a value or a belief. But say your cat just ate the center out of your 300-year-old Persian rug that's been in your family for the past five generations. Upon finding your cat and the ruined rug, you might not chuckle and say, "Oh well, after all, it was 300 years old. Nothing lasts forever." You might well look at your cat and say, "You little $%^&. I am going to KILL you." No one in my circle of friends would blame you.

Now you do yours. Using the blank form on the next page, take the time to complete an inventory of your own. I'll wait right here.

Values and Beliefs	Qualities and Traits
—	—
—	—
—	—
—	—
—	—
—	—
—	—
—	—
—	—
—	—
—	—

A Profound Exercise and a Profound Question

The question now becomes: How do I show my true self to my suspects, prospects, and customers so that I can become the competitive weapon of choice in the ways that I have described? Do I consistently show my unique value? Am I really purposeful in my sales approach? Am I trustworthy and honest at all times? Do I do as I say I will? Do I actually show my intuitive ways, and am I knowledgeable?

Truth be told, if I fall short of living and showing my unique value to my suspects, prospects, and customers, I lose my strongest competitive advantage—myself. Once I identify those words, I know I have to live up to those values.

Product Value

I developed the following Value Inventory Exercise while consulting for a *Fortune* 100 company. It seems simple, but don't underestimate its power.

In the first step of this exercise, I suggest you select your best existing customer. If you don't have any customers, you'll have to get your sales manager to let you interview another salesperson's best customer. As a last resort, if you really can't get your hands on any best existing customers and you don't have a sales manager, you can create a value inventory for your best prospect.

Step 1: Select Your Best Existing Customer(s) or Best Prospect(s)

- Sort this list by industry/niche.
- Rank and place your best customers/prospects at the top of each industry/niche list.
- From this list, select the one customer/prospect to whom you've delivered, or have the potential of delivering, the greatest hard and/or soft value.

Value has nothing to do with the amount of business you've received, or have the potential of receiving.

Hard-dollar value. It's not hard to identify this positive, tangible, easy-to-observe, and measurable result. Hard-dollar value is dollars earned, dollars saved, time saved in critical processes or deadlines, and so on. Hard-dollar value is measurable impact that your solution has had, or has the possibility of having, on this organization's top, middle, or bottom line. Hard-dollar value can be expressed using numbers or percentages.

Soft-dollar value. Positive results are derived from intangibles that are difficult to observe and measure. Soft-dollar value reflects things like shifts in attitude, lower risk, less stress/worries, guarantees, performance bonds, greater image/recognition, and so forth. Soft-dollar value can be expressed using descriptive words and phrases.

Step 2: Interview and Establish Your Value Inventory

Now, ask yourself or have a peer or your manager ask you the following three questions:

1. How long have you been servicing/working with this customer/prospect?

> IMPORTANT: Compile very detailed written notes—or record all answers at length on a cassette recorder and have them transcribed.

2. What products, services, and solutions have you been providing or are you planning to provide?
3. For each product, service, and solution answer the following:
   - What positive impact* has your product, service, or solution had (or has the potential of having) on this organization's top (revenue-generating) line? What has been the gain? Hard-dollar value? Soft-dollar value?
   - What positive impact* has your product, service, or solution had (or has the potential of having) on its middle (expense) line? What has been the gain? Hard-dollar value? Soft-dollar value?
   - What positive impact* has your product, service, or solution had (or has the potential of having) on its bottom (gross, net margin, or profit) line? What has been the gain? Hard-dollar value? Soft-dollar value?
   - Has your product, service, or solution had (or could it have) an impact on this customer's/prospect's customers? Hard- and/or soft-dollar value?
   - Has your customer/prospect experienced (or could it experience) any positive impact on the quality of its product, service, or solution, or any part of its quality process?
   - Has your customer/prospect experienced (or could it experience) any end-product enhancements? Technical edge?
   - Has your customer/prospect experienced (or could it experience) any competitive edge in pricing?
   - Has your customer/prospect experienced (or could it experience) any competitive edge in its industry position?
   - What impact* has your product, service, or solution had (or could it have) on the customer's/prospect's critical processes? Are they better? More accurate? Being done with less cost/labor? Less expensive?
   - What impact* has your product, service, or solution had (or will it have) on any of this customer's/prospect's critical, special, or ongoing projects?
   - What impact* has your product, service, or solution had (or could it have) on any aspect of this prospect's/customer's supply chain?

*Remember, in all cases *impact* and *results* must be defined in terms of hard- and/or soft-dollar value.

Now, add any questions that are specific to your customer's/prospect's industry and the results that your product, service, and/or solution provides, or has the potential to provide.

With every answer, be sure you quantify the exact impact with numbers, percentages, and time frames, or use descriptive words and phrases.

Avoid the use of insider jargon or language. Keep your answers focused in the area of business impact, not technology or systems impact.

Step 3: Develop Bullets

Take your detailed notes or audiotape transcription and create text bullets—a series of one or two sentences that describe each and every element of hard and soft value being delivered. It's best to keep these bullets as short, direct, and to the point as possible.

Step 4: Develop a Headline

Take your most impressive two or three bullets and create up to a 30-word narrative that when read by a prospect that fits your TIP (see Chapter One), is likely to elicit a "tell me more" response.

As we proceed through the rest of this book, you'll be using all of these bullets to craft concise written messages and verbal impact statements that will definitely be of interest to the Approvers, Decision Makers, Recommenders, and Influencers you encounter in the target organization.

Do It!

Complete these exercises before you move on to the next chapter. If you're experiencing any initial skepticism about what I'm suggesting here or you've simply never done anything like this before, for crying out loud, just get over it!

If necessary, track down your actual customers and ask how what you've been working on has affected operations there. Ask for estimates of specific performance levels over specific periods of time. Ask for permission to incorporate these estimates into your sales materials, and then provide all necessary confirming materials so your contact can approve what you'll be circulating.

Do these exercises before you proceed any further in the book.

> If you are hesitant because of a well-founded suspicion that there may not be any success stories to speak of in your customer base, or a fear that if you were to call most of your current customers to go over the details of your product or service, they might act to cancel the account when reminded that they're doing business with you, then you've got bigger problems than not wanting to make cold calls. Fortunately, those problems can be solved easily by updating your resume and finding another company to sell for!

Congratulations!

You've just taken the first few steps to working more efficiently and effectively. And you have created a solid list of benefits for whatever it is you're selling. I can pretty much guarantee that this list of hard and soft value you just created is the only list of its kind in your organization. Don't misplace it. In just a few more chapters, you'll be using what you just created to launch a cold-call-free, over-quota performance.

Two Big Ideas

1. Complete your Personal Value Inventory.

2. Complete your Product/Service Value Inventory.

Don't forget to go to: www.stopcoldcalling.info for additional for-fee information on this chapter that will assist you in creating your Personal and Product Value Inventories. Click on "Chapter Four: Online Assets."

Notes

NO COLD-CALLING
PRINCIPLE 5

"Never reinvent
anything that's relevant."

—E8486

Battle Plans

VERY SUCCESSFUL SALESPERSON I'VE EVER MET WHO HAS SOMETHING worthwhile to sell has an overall tactical plan, a set of steps that sets out exactly how the person plans to move products, services, and solutions to the marketplace.

You're no exception. You have to have a plan, too, if you want to win business without making cold calls.

To build your personal plan, or at least an initial draft, you will need to find out what your organization's current strategic plans are for the marketplace it serves. Any good VP of marketing and sales can and will share this plan with you if you ask.

If you're working for a company that doesn't have the marketing resources to create a full-fledged strategic plan, then you should follow the instructions in this chapter and reverse-engineer to identify the informal plan that's in place now.

> *You must be completely familiar with your company's strategic plans.* Your own roadmap to overachievement must be based on that of the company for which you work. If the two plans are headed in opposite directions, there's a problem somewhere.

Advertising

What does your company plan in this area? What is it planning to pay for? What is the company doing now? Does it use trade journal, magazine, newspaper, television, or radio advertising? Does it skip advertising altogether? Try to find a way to track down a copy of each advertising and promotional piece.

You'll need all of this to create the touch points we'll be discussing in the next chapter.

- If your advertising runs on television, get a video tape.
- If your outfit buys radio spots, get an audio tape.
- If you run ads or publish articles, get reprints.

For now, just gather them up, and keep everything on file.

Direct Mail

In the past, direct mail was used primarily for selling commodity items, such as magazine subscriptions, supplies, and homebased services. Now, even with all of the regulatory initiatives out there, all sorts of items are sold through the mail, up to and possibly including your competition's products, services, and solutions.

Whatever your company is doing or has done in the past with direct mail, get all the copies of this stuff you can and file them.

Possible Mailing Lists

Has your organization conducted customer conferences and/or seminars? Has it sponsored special customer appreciation outings, such as ball games, gatherings, or focus groups? Has your organization had a booth at trade shows or conventions? If so, who has attended? What mailing lists exist?

Don't worry if the lists are old. Get your hands on them and put them in your file.

Meet the Press

Media relations is another important area to investigate. Find out about articles on your company in magazines and newspapers. It sure makes it easier to sell if you can walk into a first meeting with a suspect, prospect, or customer and pull out a positive article from a major newspaper or the most important trade magazine in your industry.

Get hold of these, and place them in your file.

The Customer Counts!

One final point to consider can be summed up in a simple (but too frequently overlooked) question: What are you doing to keep your current customers happy and up-to-date?

> Customer service is certainly part of any smart marketing campaign. After all, how your company treats its customers after the sale will determine how much repeat business it gets. Similarly, marketing to current customers can pay hefty dividends.

So ask yourself:
- How is your organization keeping its existing customers better informed and happy?
- What kind of service are customers actually receiving?
- Who in your organization is responsible for making sure customers are getting the very best treatment possible, whether over the phone, on paper, or in person?
- What are your organization's plans to improve the level of service your customers receive?
- Does your organization have a customer newsletter?
- Does your organization sponsor focus groups and/or user groups?

Your Tactical Plan

By the time you reach the end of this book, you'll be able to complete your tactical plan, but for now be sure to include the following elements in your first draft:

1. The specific industry makeup of your territory (if applicable).
2. The demographics of likely customers you will encounter. (Use the TIP that you created earlier.)
3. A list of your current customers (if you've got customers). Outline both the current products and services each customer purchases, and add ideas for future business with each customer.
4. A summary of your current required activity levels. This should be based on your closing ratios (or the closing average in your company, if you're new). How many suspects must you typically contact to create a prospect? How many prospects must you approach and/or present your products, services, and solutions to before one becomes a customer? Closing ratios change from time to time, based on all sorts of factors, including pricing, competition, new product releases, and, of course, your own effectiveness as a salesperson.
5. A sales forecast. Make your own realistic estimates of your performance, based on all of the previous points you've developed. Sales managers love this part of the plan. Even if your estimate is a little lower than your target or quota, at least you've taken responsibility for making things happen. (And you'll look like a hero when you do exceed your target.)
6. A short narrative outlining the current state of your territory. Don't slam your predecessor with negative comments about his or her lack of effort or being "asleep at the switch." And don't complain with subtle critiques or comments on the "anemic" appearance of your territory.

Take some time to work up your plan. Do it right, and don't cut corners. Then present it to your sales manager. Review it every quarter, and update it whenever it seems appropriate to do so.

Check Your File

Take a moment right now to review the list above and to confirm that you have assembled all the materials you need before moving on to Part II of this book. When you finally do track down all this important information, ask yourself:

1. What ideas from my company's strategic plan should I be taking advantage of?
2. What do the industries and prospects that fit my TIP have in common?
3. Are there groups of suspects and prospects that these materials target that I missed in my TIP, groups that I should be targeting, too?

Once you have done all the research necessary to answer these questions, find some way to reward yourself. You deserve it.

Trust me. All this upfront work really will save you untold hours of wasted time and ill-directed work and put at your disposal many thousands of dollars' worth of high-powered marketing ideas.

Five Big Ideas

1. Take the time to review and understand your company's marketing/sales plan.

2. Understand on a fundamental level exactly how your customers will use and benefit from what you have to offer.

3. Take the time to track down every bit of marketing material your organization has developed that relates, even remotely, to what you sell for a living.

4. Review all of this material carefully, adapting what you can to your own needs.

5. Develop the first draft of your detailed, written, personalized selling plan. (You'll create the final draft once you finish this book.)

II

Getting Your
Message Across

IN PART I THE STAGE WAS SET FOR YOUR PROSPECTING EFFORTS BY GATHER-
ing critical information. You'll be using that information in this
part of the book to craft specific messages for specific people.

   If you haven't done the work in Part I, don't bother reading
Part II.

NO COLD-CALLING
PRINCIPLE 6

"PR stands for:

Promote Regularly."

—E8486

Buzz

OVER THE YEARS I'VE TRIED A GOOD MANY WAYS TO GET MY OWN DISTINCTIVE message out to everyone in my territory who fits my TIP.

The message I am speaking of is one that promotes in a positive way what you can (and can't) do for the companies and individuals in your sales territory. Please understand, this is much, much different than focusing on what your organization is (or perhaps isn't) doing at this very moment. What we're talking about is generating what the marketing people call *buzz*—about what you can deliver.

If you happen to read anything in this chapter (or anywhere else in this book) that causes you to say or think: *Hey, I tried something like that once before, and it didn't work,* do me a favor. Bite your tongue, push that negative thought away, and do what I am suggesting anyway—as it's described here, not as you remember doing it before. The ideas you read about in the pages that follow will work over the long haul if you give them an honest try and follow the directions you read here. The bottom line is: This stuff is bulletproof.

Seven Ways to Build Buzz

Here are seven buzz-building ideas that *won't* cost you a penny, and *will*, without a doubt, help you generate positive word of mouth in your territory. Your aim here is to determine the best untapped avenues of opportunity for you to get your word out within your territory.

Idea 1: Get Free Media Coverage

Don't limit your thinking. You can and should exploit the following avenues:

- College campus radio stations
- College campus newspapers
- Local business and financial talk radio
- Internet business talk shows (There's a great one at www.selling acrossamerica.com.)
- Local newspapers (business section)
- Local business journals
- Industry-specific newsletters and e-zines
- Association-specific newsletters and e-zines

I strongly invite you to develop a punchy, straight-to-the-point press release that highlights some genuinely newsworthy aspect of your product, service, or solution. Mail out ten of these a week and follow up by phone as your schedule permits. The closer your release matches up with the actual house style of the journal or broadcast outlet you send it to, the more likely it is to appear verbatim. Check out the sample shown in Figure 6.1.

Idea 2: Take Advantage of Your Company's Personalities

If you sell for a company that has a board of directors, get the list of names of those who are currently on the board of your company. If any of your executives serve on some other company's board of directors, get the names of those companies. Add them to your list of potential contacts.

Speaking of your company's top executives, find out if they know other individuals in your territory with similar titles. Ask what colleges

FIGURE 6.1: Sample Press Release

FOR IMMEDIATE RELEASE   For further information,
                                                        media@sellingacrossamerica.com

SECRETS OF SELLING ACROSS AMERICA REVEALED

SAN DIEGO, CA: Figures show that 75 percent of salespeople do not meet their sales quota because they are getting appointments with the wrong people, according to noted *Wall Street Journal* bestselling author and the nation's leading sales expert, Anthony Parinello. What makes matters worse is that when salespeople finally get the appointment, they use the wrong language!

"Organizations have all but stopped training their salespeople because of budget cutbacks, but salespeople can take action quickly and turn things around." Parinello suggests that salespeople focus on making each sale larger, cutting the time it takes to sell, and ensuring that each existing customer buys the add-ons that provide higher-margin sales.

A salesperson must become more of a businessperson. They have to start speaking their clients' language, which, as Parinello points out, is tailored to four individuals: the language of functions with the Recommender, features for the Influencer, advantages to engage the Decision Maker, and benefits to break the preoccupation of the Approver.

"Stop closing the sales," Parinello suggests. "Opening a business relationship is much more meaningful and powerful than any closing techniques of yesteryear. Let's face it, you don't shake someone's hand with a closed fist, and you don't hug someone with crossed arms."

Anthony Parinello is the author of five books on this subject, including *The Wall Street Journal* bestseller *Think and Sell Like a CEO*, the renowned *Selling to VITO: The Very Important Top Officer*, and *Getting the Second Appointment*. Parinello has 28 years of sales and marketing experience. His tactics are used by 65 of the *Fortune* 100 companies, and he has personally trained over one million people.

Parinello's words of sales wisdom can be heard every Friday on his newly launched Internet talk-radio show, "Selling Across America." Guests are luminaries in the sales training industry, including: Tom Hopkins, David McNally, Warren Greshes, Dr. Tony Alessandra, Glenna Salsbury, and Nance Rosen.

Listen to his show on www.sellingacrossamerica.com.

# # # # # # # # # #

they graduated from, what clubs and associations they belong to, and what charitable events they're active in.

Idea 3: Take Advantage of Your Company's Community Relations Activities

If your company is sponsoring any community event—charitable or commercial—you should get involved.

Whether it's a fundraiser, a food drive, a golf tournament, or a 10K run, you owe it to yourself to participate—and meet and greet. Get eyeball-to-eyeball, press the flesh, and get face-to-face.

Idea 4: Take Advantage of Suppliers and Business Partners

What companies in your territory supply goods and services to your own organization or to any of your customers? Understand, when I say your customers, that includes any customers that your organization has.

Identify at least five such companies you can reach out to.

Idea 5: Take Advantage of Related, Noncompetitive Organizations

What are the noncompetitive organizations that can lead you to opportunities in your territory? You can generate buzz by reaching out to them.

For example, if you sell commercial carpeting and provide interior design services, a noncompetitive organization would be global moving and storage companies that relocate companies into your territory. In this case the noncompetitive organization does not fit your TIP: however, the companies that they can introduce you to—and talk you up to—will fit your TIP.

Idea 6: Take Advantage of Your Advocacy Lists

These are scrupulously maintained contact lists that by definition are constantly in a state of flux. They contain the names, telephone numbers, physical addresses, and e-mail addresses of each and every person in your territory who wants to see you get to the next highest level in your profession and is a great supporter of you and your products, services, and solutions. In other words, these are the people who will coach and mentor you to greater success. What's in it for them? Simple: the law of reciprocity. (They help you, you help them, they help you, you help them, and on and on.) Typically, these are upwardly mobile individuals.

Advocacy lists work best if you divide your list into four parts:

1. *The "A" list.* These are individuals you know in high places. They can be family members, friends, clergy, customers, and/or individuals who run the company you work for. My "A" list currently has 22 names. These are the names of my biggest supporters. Some are my friends, others are CEOs, still others are salespeople and alumni of my seminars. Don't ever forget or underestimate the power of the individuals who run the organization you work for. When is the last time you talked to your CEO or president? Do they know anyone in one or more of the organizations in your territory?

2. *The "B" list.* These are individuals and/or organizations that have given you a referral during the current sales year. They're people you've followed up with. They can be suspects who have never bought from you, prospects, or more likely longstanding customers. Do any of these folks know of someone (who knows someone who knows someone…) who can quickly be recruited to be a coach and/or mentor of your efforts at any one of the organizations in your territory?

3. *The "C" list.* These are all the board members (or equivalents) of your current customers. The most powerful name-drop you can use when looking for a coach and/or mentor in a target organization in your territory is the name of a current or past board member or other high-level player. Identify and be ready to connect with the people on this list—they have extraordinary networking skills and resources.

4. *The "D" list.* These are individuals in associations and groups that you belong to and are currently active in.

These lists can help you in quickly identifying someone (or a bunch of someones) as coaches and mentors in any suspect or prospect organization in your territory. But you have to set up the lists if you want to generate buzz with them.

Idea 7: Take Advantage of Everybody Else!
No joke. Be ready to generate buzz by connecting with:

- your alumni association.
- your favorite teachers, professors, and clergy.

- your own family's inner circle. (I recently found out that one of my relatives knows a very senior executive at the largest computer company in the world.)
- people you happen to be sitting next to at the ball game. (It's totally possible and probable that the people who happen to be sitting next to you need your products, services, and solutions.)

OK, you get the point. Nothing, no place, and no one is sacred when it comes to making connections and generating buzz.

Seven Big Ideas

1. Get free media coverage.

2. Take advantage of your company's personalities.

3. Take advantage of your company's community relations activities.

4. Take advantage of suppliers and business partners.

5. Take advantage of related, noncompetitive organizations.

6. Take advantage of your advocacy lists.

7. Take advantage of everybody else.

Notes

NO COLD-CALLING PRINCIPLE 7

"F-words (facts, features, functions) only appeal to a few prospects."

—E8486

Sales Heaven, Sales Hell

THE FOLLOWING DEFINITIONS ARE TRUE FOR ALL SALESPEOPLE:

Sales Heaven: a place where you make sales
Sales Hell: a place where you lose sales

There are four principles of the all-important first contact in sales. When followed, these four principles will ensure that you spend more of your time in Sales Heaven and avoid even the shortest of stays in Sales Hell or anyplace close to it. Each of these principles revolves around the word *pitch*.

What I mean by *pitch* is the function, feature, advantage, and/or benefit of your product, service, and/or solution that you can most profitably highlight for this suspect or prospect. The pitch is the part of what you offer that has the highest likelihood of being interesting to that specific person.

The pitch is not the "how" of your approach. We'll get to that later. The question now is: What parts of your company's activities are worth customizing to a specific individual's interests?

This is a question mediocre salespeople never bother to ask themselves.

> Such customizing may seem like a minor issue, but stop and think for a moment about how tiny the margin of error is that separates success and failure.

Consider the difference between the first-place winner of the game, contest, or competition and the team or person who comes in second. In many cases the margin is so vanishingly small that it can barely be measured. In the world of sports, it can be one-hundredth of a second or the fraction of an inch that makes the difference between making or missing a single putt, goal, slam dunk, or run. But how vast the difference in rewards for those who come in first and those who come in second.

The salesperson of the day, week, month, quarter, half year, or year may win by only one sale. That winning sale often boils down to one winning presentation. That one presentation may boil down to having made a good impression on a single prospect. That one prospect boils down to one suspect. And one suspect boils down to one sales touch, and that touch is a PITCH.

Critical Sales Definitions

You may or may not be familiar with the concepts of function, feature, advantage, and benefit in selling. Whether you're a novice or a veteran, please take a moment to review these concepts now.

Function

This is how your customers use whatever it is you're selling. The function of your product, service, or solution is reflected in how the individual and/or organization will change procedures, practices, and processes as a direct result of your stuff. It's typically what's found in the owner's manual.

Example

Let's say you sell consumable supplies for tanning salons. The functions of your consumables would include how the user mixes the tanning solution and fills the airbrush equipment, how the user applies these solutions, how long it takes to dry, and how long it will be before the next application is necessary. The functions of what you sell may require the user to attend special and somewhat complex training. In the simplest case, the user may just read the owner's manual that accompanies whatever you sold them. That's the function—the how.

Feature(s)

This is the answer to the question: What's under the hood of what you sell? What pieces, components, and parts are contained in it? What are your product's, service's, and solution's technical qualifications? What is the stated performance? When you answer these questions, you'll have your feature set sitting in front of you.

Example

If you sell copiers, the features would be the list of specifications on your data sheets. At what speed does it cruise while making copies? Does it collate and staple? Make color copies? How many copies will it make before it needs maintenance? How much power does it consume? The list of features probably goes on and on. Generally speaking, most of what we sell is feature rich. Avoid the trap of selling features to everyone. Features are not of equal interest to everyone in the target organization.

Most salespeople are experts on features. We've been bombarded with product training and been told that we must be product experts. That's both a blessing and a curse. Being singularly focused on anything in life is not healthy, and that certainly goes for salespeople who are singularly focused on the details of their products or services.

Advantages

Looking for the advantages of what you sell can be a bit tricky. Over the years, the best way I've found to do this is to answer a simple but powerful question: "What edge will my product give this customer?"

You see, advantages change with every customer. That's why they're so tricky. Functions and features are pretty much product-centric, but advantages are customer-centric. When you answer this question for *this* unique prospect (which may take a couple of discussions and/or visits), you'll have the real advantages of what it is you happen to be selling that speaks to *this* person or organization on how *they* can get an edge. In the early stages of the process, you are basically *auditioning* possible advantages that may or may not resonate with *this* person.

Example

If you happen to be selling payroll outsourcing services to small- to medium-size manufacturing organizations in your territory, your list of advantages could look something like this:

- It will be able to provide greater accuracy for its employee salary tracking, which will give it more up-to-date, timely, and accurate information on its job-cost accounting system, which will allow it to bill customers more accurately and cover its own cost more completely.
- It will save additional time and money since these services will allow the existing cost accounting department to do other, more important tasks.
- In addition, outsourcing will relieve this customer of the headaches of worrying about state and federal compliance and workers' compensation insurance issues.

Did you notice how the list of advantages has a soft side to it? Advantages are tailored to the customer. They address more than the generic needs that this customer may have.

Benefit(s)

Looking for the benefit is even more difficult than articulating the advantages. Difficult? Yes. But impossible? No.

By definition, a benefit is the actual direct (tangible) and/or indirect (intangible) result that this customer will get from the use of your product, service, and/or solution. Look closely at the key words for us to consider, the words that will take us to the list of benefits. They are: *direct/tangible results* and *indirect/intangible business results*. Bottom line: Think of stuff you can measure (direct/tangible results) or quantify by comparing it to what was experienced or achieved before you came on the scene (indirect/intangible results). Unlike the advantages, benefits are all about business performance—what actually happened with similar customers.

Example

Let's say for the moment that you're selling a piece of software that improves Web site performance and Web site marketing. The direct/tangible results might look something like this:

· Increased revenue up to 12 percent
· Increased market share by as much as 4 percent
· Lower expenses to 45 percent

The indirect/intangible results may include:
· Greater brand awareness
· Greater recognition in the marketplace
· Getting a leg up on the competition
· Greater referrals
· Testimonials to other markets

As you can see, benefits tend to be business-centric, not product- or customer-centric. That's why they can be challenging to identify.

Make Your Benefits Even More Powerful

Warning: Guiding principle ahead.

Because results that are either tangible or intangible are desirable to key people within your target organization, and because those people tend to be short on time, it's a good idea to *introduce the element of time whenever you emphasize the benefits that your product, service, or solution has to offer.*

The time I am referring to is not the implementation time your technical people identify, but the amount of time it typically takes this type of customer to realize the benefit you have identified.

How long will it take this customer to post the 12 percent revenue boost? How long will it be before they increase market share by 4 percent and lower expenses by 45 percent?

> IMPORTANT: If you have a proven track record of delivering these results in an unbelievable time frame (say, three months), then you might want to give a four- to six-month estimate. It's always best to understate and overdeliver.

Now that you've got the definitions of function, feature, advantage, and benefit under your belt, you're ready to explore the Seven Touch Points of the Sale that are the foundation of this book.

Don't stop here.

Keep reading.

Four Big Ideas

1. Be ready to identify and discuss your functions.

2. Be ready to identify and discuss your features.

3. Be ready to identify and discuss advantages.

4. Be ready to identify and discuss your benefits.

Don't forget to go to: www.stopcoldcalling.info for additional for-fee information on this chapter. Click on "Chapter Seven: Online Assets."

Notes

NO COLD-CALLING
PRINCIPLE 8

"Everything picks up speed
when it goes downhill."

—E8486

CHAPTER EIGHT

The Seven Touch Principles of the Sale

T HROUGHOUT THE DAY (AND SOMETIMES INTO THE EVENING) MY PHONE rings with calls generated by people I don't want to talk to—people who are making cold calls and who know absolutely nothing about me.

Of course, it's not limited to phone calls. Often I'll receive a fax, e-mail, or snail-mail message about a product, service, or solution that I have absolutely no use for or interest in. I call this *junkyard selling*.

Junk calls. Junk mail. Junk faxes. Junk e-mail. All of it is a waste of precious time, energy, and attention on the part of both the salesperson and the person who receives the message. Perhaps the most perplexing thought of all is this: I do have definite and immediate needs for services in my business and personal life, things that I have allocated a budget for, things that I must seek out, evaluate, and invest in.

Why, then, can't the right salespeople selling the right products, services, and solutions find me?

ANSWER: Because virtually all salespeople are COLD-CALLING. Because virtually all salespeople are selling without a TIP. Because they didn't read this book.

Seven Principles

A touch is really the opposite of a cold call. In the process of reviewing the material in this chapter, I think you will confirm for yourself that if you follow this system, you really will be able to avoid making cold calls for as long as you are in sales.

> In this chapter, we'll take a close look at the "what," "when," "who," and "how" principles of the sales touch. The touch is your customized, researched, carefully considered contact strategy for contacting people who are predisposed to buy. The touch can make all the difference in your career, the difference between finishing the race as the winner you were meant to be, and the second-place finish you're hoping the competition turns in.

Touch Principle 1: Know What to Pitch—and Know That Not Everyone Needs to Know Everything

Before you go running out the door to make a sales call, before you pick up the phone, before you compose the text of your next mass e-mailing, please realize that each and every person you contact and make an attempt to sell to does not necessarily need to know each function, feature, advantage, or benefit you have to offer.

As a matter of fact, some individuals in your territory are predisposed in their need to know, while others are preopposed in their need to know.

Here's a simple table that will help you master this extremely important concept:

Role*	Predisposed	Preopposed
Approver of Your Sale	Benefits	Functions and Features
Decision Maker of Your Sale	Advantages	Functions and Features
Influencer of Your Sale	Features and Functions	Benefits
Recommender of Your Sale	Functions	Benefits

* See Chapter Two.

Do you see the trend here? There is a decided split between one subgroup, the Approver and the Decision Maker, and the other subgroup, and the Influencer and the Recommender.

Here is this book's main point condensed into a single sentence:

> *When in doubt, follow the guidelines in the table above in all of your communications—written, verbal, smoke signal, whatever—to sales prospects.*

In more than 20 years of selling, the guidelines have not failed me— not once. Follow this rule religiously, and you will get into Sales Heaven. Ignore it, and you will wind up in Sales Hell!

But Tony, how do I know what role someone has?

This is a lot easier than you would imagine. And you won't need to reach for your Ouija board for help. The first option: *Make an intelligent assumption* based on your own experience in the industry. This is usually good enough to get you in the door, as we shall see a little later. Then you can *ask an intelligent question* once you finally do get in the door. Ask, "What role do you play in the procurement of (encapsulate what your product does and say it here)?" Note that you don't describe what your product *is*, but rather what the product *does*. Based on the answer you get, make an assumption as to what the person's role is. We'll cover the details of the questions you should ask in a later chapter. For now, just remember that memorizing and implementing the table above is your key to Sales Heaven.

Touch Principle 2: Know When to Pitch

It's often said that timing is everything. That certainly applies to our No Cold-Calling selling model.

The Bible had it right: To everything there really is a cycle or season. This applies to nature, humanity, our careers, the products, the services,

65

and the solutions we sell, as well as the approach we take to the organizations that fit our TIP.

It is a huge mistake to approach a prospective customer at the wrong or inopportune time. A message that's powerful and memorable can quickly become a distant memory if it arrives at the wrong time.

> **Example**
>
> If you're selling in the retail environment and you represent a spring line, it would be downright foolish to approach your prospects in the spring with the hope of making an immediate sale. You're late. Your prospects needed to place their orders months ago.

You could, however, show up on your prospect's doorstep with an idea or two on how to sell the dickens out of their current line. What will this do for you? It will put you in the position of being a trusted advisor, a thought partner. And once you achieve that status, you will get the wallet share that you deserve.

Cycles. Organizations have cycles of needs. These cycles follow the Approver's strategic goals and visions. The Approver's strategic goals and visions typically follow the industry trends. Industry trends are everywhere. And the easiest way for you and me to dial into these cycles of needs is to read the industry publications, follow the relevant Web sites, and then follow this four-step process:

1. *Ask yourself:* Does your own organization use whatever it is that you sell? If your answer is "no," then go to Step 4.
2. *Ask yourself:* If your organization had to purchase its own product, who would be involved in that buying process in the categories of Recommender, Influencer, Decision Maker, Approver? Get their titles!
3. *Sit down and interview* your own organization's Recommender(s), Influencer(s), Decision Maker, and Approver, and get answers to

the following questions. (Everywhere you see "_____," fill in your product, service, and/or solution.)
- What time or year/month is the need highest for "_____"?
- What would be the consequence of not having "_____" at that time?

4. *Sit down and interview* your organization's best customers (in every industry/niche or subgroup [see Chapter Four] who played the role of Recommender(s), Influencer(s), Decision Maker, and Approver), and get answers to the following questions. (Everywhere you see "_____," fill in your product, service, and/or solution.)
- What time or year/month is the need highest for "_____"?
- What would be the consequence of not having "_____" at that time?

Depending upon the industry/niche or subgroup and the role of the individual, you'll always be able to find someone whose timing for what you sell is perfect! Trust me—the combinations are endless.

Touch Principle 3: Know Whom to Pitch

There are, of course, only four role categories of individuals you can pitch to.

There are many reasons salespeople give to justify their choice of whom they will pitch. At the end of the day, these justifications boil down to the following (self-limiting and career-limiting) fact: When we're not challenged to do otherwise, we like to stay in our comfort zone. We tend to feel most comfortable in a sales situation when we feel safe—that is, when we:
- know what to say.
- know what questions may come up.
- know the answers to the questions that may come up.
- know that our chances are slim to none that we will get rejected.

This is exactly why more than 90 percent of all salespeople will consciously ignore the Approver, spend little time with the Decision Maker, camp out with the Influencers, and become friends with Recommenders.

If you want to get the rewards most salespeople get, just keep following these rules.

If you want different rewards, use this book to challenge yourself and set up a new strategy.

Touch Principle 4: Know Where to Pitch

Whenever I look out my window of opportunity into the industries, niches, and subgroups in my territory that fit my TIP, I see a specific order. That order tells me whom to pitch first, second, third, and fourth in any company I target.

This sequence has been responsible for my success in selling bigger deals in less time without making cold calls. I challenge you to follow this sequence:

1. Pitch the Approver first.
2. Pitch the Influencer second.
3. Pitch the Recommender third.
4. Pitch the Decision Maker fourth.

Why follow this order? Let me answer that question by posing another one: Who in any organization knows *everything* that's going on? Who in every organization is most concerned about everything? Who ultimately owns the balance sheet?

Yep, it's the Approver. And what's more, the Approver is not the least bit shy about telling you where to go and with whom to talk. Approvers will tell you honestly if you stand a chance of doing business with their organizations. They'll even tell you whether they'll eventually approve your business relationship with their firm—and you can take their answers to the bank.

Got enough reasons for starting at the top?

Pitching the Influencers next will give you tremendous insights as to the fit of your products, services, and solutions to their needs.

Getting an audience with the Recommender(s) will confirm what you've learned with the Influencer and provide food for thought about any value-added functions you may be able to provide as part of your solution.

Putting the Decision Maker next will get him or her to endorse what's been discovered. Remember, the Decision Maker must say "yes" to someone—and if you play your cards right, that someone will be you.

Touch Principle 5: Know Why to Ask

Why do salespeople need to ask questions? Because salespeople need to listen.

You need to listen because you *can't learn anything when you're talking.*

On my talk show, *Selling Across America* (www.sellingacrossamerica. com), I've interviewed some of our nation's greatest teachers of listening skills and needs-probing. What I've come to learn is how very important it is to know why you are asking a question. This is just as important as the content of the question itself.

There's a lot to understand when it comes to honing your questioning skills. For now, all I want you to remember is that the point of any touch is to learn stuff about the other person and about the company you're targeting—not to talk.

Touch Principle 6: Know How to Pitch

If you've got one boilerplate speech that you give again and again without any variation to people you've just met, if your presentation contains only minimal customization or research, or if what you say or communicate about your company is not based *primarily* on the particular organization and the person you're targeting, then you're not going to reach your maximum potential as a salesperson. That's a guarantee.

Salespeople ask me all the time whether it's really necessary to do customized research for each and every new person they connect with. I always give the same answer:

You've got a choice between winging the deal and winning the deal.

I've always preferred the latter, and I hope you do, too! And make no mistake—winning the deal begins with the research you do before you talk to someone.

Touch Principle 7: Know the Modalities

There are three primary learning styles or learning preferences that all people adhere to. What preference does your targeted suspect/prospect have? Being able to answer this question sooner rather than later in the relationship will help you to make sure that your suspect/prospect gets the most from any message you send.

Learning modalities are actually pretty easy to spot, if you know what to look for. Here's a quick rundown:

1. Visual learning style/preference: *"Seeing is believing!"*
2. Auditory learning style/preference: *"I hear what you're saying!"*
3. Kinesthetic learning style/preference: *"I've got a good feeling about this!"*

Clues and Cues

Visual learners have certain easy-to-identify habits. They frequently use words that key into their preference for visual information. You'll find that individuals who are visual tend to make statements like:

- "I don't get the picture."
- "Get the picture?"
- "Can't you just see it?"
- "Here's my point of view on this. . ." (Don't be surprised if this person wants to sketch or doodle something for you. Have pads handy for such an opportunity: one with lines and one without. Always ask: *"Which one would you prefer?"* Nine times out of ten the visual individual will pick the one without the lines.)
- "Why don't you just show me?"
- "Imagine this. . ."
- "That's brilliant!"
- And the all-time classic: *"I had a vision."*

Words like *brilliant, flash, show,* and *see* are more likely to have a greater impact on a visual person than on people in the other two categories, as are visual aids and diagrams. Remember: If they can't see it, they won't believe it.

Auditory learners love to listen to the words that are being said and the way that the entire message is being delivered. The auditory is likely to use words and phrases like:

- "Listen to this. . ."
- "Let me tell you. . ."
- "Let me ask you this. . ."
- "My question is. . ."
- "My opinion is. . ."
- "Tell me. . ."
- "I want you to hear from my vice president. . ."
- And the all-time classic: *"Tune your ears on to this!"*

Folks who have a strong auditory preference will be extremely sensitive to the pitch, tone, and volume of your voice. You must never use a droning monotone when speaking to an auditory learner. This is a bad idea in general, but it is the kiss of death when interacting with someone for whom speech and hearing is the primary channel for communication.

Always modulate your voice and avoid any sing-song style that incorporates only two or three vocal "notes." Pause—for a good two seconds or longer—when making an important point. Don't raise your volume when you're trying to make a point; instead, raise or lower the pitch of your voice.

Kinesthetic learners have an inherent need to get the "feel" of your message. They're usually extremely easy to identify.

Interesting side note: It's typical for the kinesthetic learner's handshake to be accompanied by a touch on the forearm; their handshake usually lasts longer than those of visual or auditory learners.

Kinesthetic learners really do like to touch, and they really do use phrases like:

- "That feels right."
- "That just doesn't feel right."
- "My gut feeling is. . ."
- "My sense is. . ."
- "I don't feel comfortable with. . ."
- "I haven't had much hands-on time with. . ."
- "How do you feel about. . ."
- And the all-time classic: *"I felt it in my fingertips."* (Or, *"I felt it all the way down to my toes."*)

Kinesthetic learners put a premium on emotional connection—feelings and person-to-person contact. They enjoy connecting on a gut level. Your challenge is to find a way to facilitate this connection on this visceral level with your ideas and strategies. Do not focus on the logic or external elements of the situations; focus on the relationship, on earning trust. Expect digressions, both on the phone and in person. Expect to be asked questions about your personal values and experience. Be as well versed as you can about the challenges this suspect/prospect might be facing (another side benefit of your TIP).

Finally, remember this: Human beings are always inclined to communicate by means of their own primary learning style. Superior salespeople—

like successful politicians—learn to overcome this inclination. Unless you are certain you are dealing with someone who shares your learning modality, overcompensate in targeting your pitch to your contact's way of accessing information.

Seven Big Ideas

1. Touch Principle 1: Know What to Pitch—and Know That Not Everyone Needs to Know Everything.

Role	Predisposed	Preopposed
Approver of Your Sale	Benefits	Functions and Features
Decision Maker of Your Sale	Advantages	Functions and Features
Influencer of Your Sale	Functions and Features	Benefits
Recommender of Your Sale	Functions	Benefits

When in doubt, follow the guidelines on how to treat the various roles in all of your communications to sales prospects—written, verbal, smoke signal, whatever.

2. Touch Principle 2: Know When to Pitch.

3. Touch Point Principle 3: Know Whom to Pitch.

4. Touch Principle 4: Know Where to Pitch.

5. Touch Principle 5: Know Why to Ask.

6. Touch Principle 6: Know How to Pitch.

7. Touch Prinicple 7: Know the Modalities.

Don't forget to go to www.stopcoldcalling.info for additional for-fee information. Click on "Chapter Eight: Online Assets."

Notes

NO COLD-CALLING
PRINCIPLE 9

"Send all of your

old correspondence

to your competition."

—E8486

Ten Powerful Ingredients for Your Correspondence

I BARELY MADE IT THROUGH HIGH-SCHOOL ENGLISH. YET SOMEHOW I'VE TAUGHT MBA graduates, sales professionals, and CEOs about writing. Go figure.

Specifically, I've taught these high-powered folks how to create correspondence that gets attention, job offers, appointments, and sales. How did I do it? By studying what business professionals read, what catches their attention, and what interests them—and then by testing what I had learned over and over and over again.

How does it work? That's exactly what you're going to find out in this chapter. Before you get started, though, I must warn you that you may not like all of what you read in the following paragraphs and pages. You may find it unorthodox in its style and approach. My advice to you now is not to let your opinions get in the way of using an extremely powerful approach that has the power to redefine the way you get appointments. If you don't use what follows, you cannot expect to develop powerful, barrier-busting, attention-getting, customized sales correspondence. And if you don't do that, you cannot expect to enjoy the benefits of my No Cold-Calling selling model.

Let the Numbers Do the Talking

By my count, there are more than 20 books currently in circulation that teach the reader how to write a business letter. The problem is, if you follow what they suggest, you'll get what everyone else is getting in terms of interest and response rates.

Typically, business letters get an average 2 to 4 percent response rate; on a good day you may get 6 percent.

So here's my question: How does 45 percent sound? How about 87 percent? How about 100 percent? These numbers are not just my own experience, but the real-world results reported by my alumni. These are individuals who work for average organizations; they have average products, services, and solutions; their sales territories are average; they report to average sales managers.

What's *not average* about the alumni who achieved these incredible results is the process they use—and their attitudes about using that process in their sales work. They took what you're about to read and put it into action.

And not only that. They punched through one or more of the following self-limiting, self-defeating, self-sabotaging mantras:

- "No one reads unsolicited mail."
- "This will look like junk mail when I'm done."
- "I am not a writer."
- "This is the marketing department's job."
- "I've tried something like this before."
- "My manager won't let me do this."
- "That's not proper style."

If you're tempted to say, think, or mutter under your breath any variation on any of the above sentiments, can it! Save the static for your kid's next science experiment—and memorize and follow the principles in this chapter.

You're about to discover ten writing motivators that will win awareness and results you never dreamed of. In the next chapter, you'll get ten specific writing examples you can build into just about any template. Then it will be up to you to deploy what you know into your written word. You may choose to send a piece of snail mail, a postcard, white paper, fax, brochure, or e-presentation. It's up to you.

Power-Writing Motivator 1: The Need to Belong to Something, Someplace, or Someone

Everyone has the need to belong to something. That's why associations, nonprofit organizations, country clubs, and fitness clubs of all types are thriving. If you've done even the most superficial reading about human motivation and psychology, you'll recall the work of Abraham Maslow (1908–1970), who accurately defined five levels of human needs. The third of these is the need to belong, and receive love and recognition. Abe's work is well founded and has been considered the genesis of many ideas on the topic of personal development.

Putting Writing Motivator 1 to Work in Your Correspondence

Whenever you create a correspondence to any suspect/prospect, you must appeal to his or her need to belong.

- Always use their title.
- Always refer to their industry.
- Always refer to their company and/or department.
- Always refer to their particular job/function/responsibility.

Power-Writing Motivator 2: The Need for Candor

Honesty is still the best policy. Be honest, even when it hurts.

Never, ever lie to a suspect/prospect (or anyone else). Sell from the heart, no matter what it takes. If you don't believe enough in what you're selling to tell the truth about it at all times, find something else to sell.

Putting Motivator 2 to Work in Your Correspondence

Honesty means not having to say you're being honest. It should—must—go without saying that you're leveling with the person to whom you're writing. Avoid the following phrases and practices and anything close to them:

- "To be perfectly honest with you. . ."
- "Honestly. . ."
- "To tell you the truth. . ."
- "I shouldn't be telling you this. . ."
- "I've been asked not to say this, but. . ."
- "I am not supposed to tell you about future products, but. . ."
- "I'll make an exception to the rule. . ."
- "I know this is breaking the rules but. . ."

Also avoid overpromising and under-delivering:

- "We have hundreds of clients in your industry."
- "Plenty of our customers tell us. . ."
- "A lot of the time we're able to. . ."
- "You'll not find this information anywhere else. . ."

By the same token, you must be careful about generalizations. Whenever quoting numbers or percentages, use phrases like:

- "by as much as X percent" or
- "up to $X."

Use a relative-ranking name-drop if you don't have permission to use a customer's or prospect's information.

- "Seven of the top ten entertainment sites. . ."
- "Fifty of San Diego's largest manufacturers. . ."
- "Twenty-eight percent of. . ."
- "The NASCAR Driver of the Year. . ."

Power-Writing Motivator 3: The Need for Integrity in One's Business Partners

To stand any chance whatsoever of turning prospects into customers, you *must* be ready, willing, and able to stand behind every word that comes out of your mouth. (This connects back to Motivator 2. If you don't tell the truth, you can't possibly broadcast integrity.)

If standing behind your commitments means losing a (short-term) customer today, so be it. You can always come back tomorrow. And when you do come back, you will be remembered as a person of integrity.

By the way, my definition of integrity is: doing *what* you said you would do, *when* you said you would do it; and if you can't do it when you said you would, *speaking up* and renegotiating the task and time frame well in advance of the deadline.

Too many salespeople (heck, too many people) seem to assume that it's bad etiquette to admit you've made a mistake. Nothing could be further from the truth.

Taking personal responsibility for your relationship with your suspects, prospects, and customers means being willing to back up and say those dreaded words: "I'm sorry," "I apologize," "That's my fault," or any of their appropriate variations when something goes wrong. Even if something doesn't go wrong and your contact is simply confused, disoriented, or in a bad mood, you should be willing to use the S word—"Sorry!"

Guess what? If you really mean it, people tend to be less mean.

Putting Motivator 3 to Work in Your Correspondence

Avoid using phrases like "If you have any questions, you can call me at. . ."

> Remember, *you* are sending the correspondence to the recipient. It's *your* job to call and find out whether your contact has any questions.

You should also avoid:

- "We might be able to. . . " (or any other rendition of a wishy-washy promise or "weasel language").
- "If I/we get a chance I'll/we'll call you. . ."
- "Assuming that. . ."
- "Let me make an assumption. . ."
- "Let me tell you. . ."

Avoid making any recommendation or offering any opinion if you do not yet understand what this person/organization wants to do. If you haven't been asked for your opinion, don't offer it in a piece of marketing correspondence. Doing so is the sales equivalent of malpractice.

Do use phrases like "I'll call you on Friday, May 14, at 9:30 A.M."

Of course, because the subject is integrity, you know full well that when you build something like this into your correspondence, you must—

repeat must—call at the prescribed time. (Actually, it's not a bad idea to call a couple of minutes early.)

Power-Writing Motivator 4: The Need to Be Able to Trust What a Business Partner Says

Earning and maintaining credibility is vitally important. It's often said that you can't get too much of a good thing. That's the way it is with credibility.

Webster's Dictionary definition of credibility is as follows:

Cred-i-bil'i-ty: *worthy of belief or confidence, trustworthy, a testimonial attesting to the bearer's right to being credible.*

Putting Motivator 4 to Work in Your Correspondence

When's the last time you asked any of your prospects and/or customers to give you a letter of recommendation—a written testimonial about your personal performance and the performance of your products, services, and solutions?

I thought so.

Before you move on to the next chapter, pick up the telephone and call the top ten percent of your current prospects (yes, prospects) and the top ten percent of your customers and ask each of them for a letter of reference. (If you don't have any customers, go to someone in your organization that does, and show him or her this page.)

Get a fistful of written letters that state just how good you really are. You'll learn how to use them a little later on.

Power-Writing Motivator 5: The Need for Quantifiable Value

The fastest way to prove your value is not by asking your suspects and prospects to read your marketing materials, but rather to tell a true story about organizations that are in a similar industry/niche or subgroup. Choose stories that this suspect/prospect can identify with.

Putting Motivator 5 to Work in Your Correspondence

Broadcast the value you deliver to your existing customers.

Broadcasting means telling your suspects/prospects that fit your TIP about verifiable success stories. Here's what I mean:

- "Our widgets worked for the fifth largest process manufacturing plant in western Texas."
- "We were able to help reduce overhead costs by as much as 12 percent last quarter, while increasing overall effectiveness."

The implication, of course, is that if your suspect/prospect should ask to speak with someone at that joint in western Texas, you'll have your name-drop's name and telephone number at the ready. Want to lose points in a hurry? When you're asked for the name, say something like: "We're not allowed to give that information out. . ." or "That's not my territory. I'll have to get the name from so and so. . ."

If you're going to use this dramatic approach to build your credibility—and I urge you to—you have to be willing to take the following steps.

1. Work with current customers to establish exactly how well (or how poorly) your product, service, or solution is actually working.
2. Once you isolate the (no doubt innumerable) customers who are thrilled with what your organization has accomplished for them, you have to quantify the level of the success they are actually experiencing.

That might mean someone (or a bunch of someones) has to be able to put a real, verifiable number on what you've done (or what your organization has done) for your customer. If your customer is willing to do the number crunching for you, that's great. In many instances, though, you'll need to ask for raw data from the customer, analyze it yourself, and submit it to your customer for approval. Yes, it takes some time, but probably not as much time as you think. The truth is that this is work you should do for all your current customers. When the budget-crunching campaign starts up at your customer's headquarters, don't you want to be able to demonstrate in no uncertain terms the value you add?

Power-Writing Motivator 6: Greed

The power of greed is awesome. I spent a good deal of time with a small group of individuals who did not in any way, shape, or form embrace, display, or exhibit any degree of greed. They were Buddhist monks at the monastery in Tembochie, a small hamlet high in the Himalayas, in the Kingdom of Nepal. If I were selling to them, I wouldn't build any correspondence around this principle. But I'm not. And neither are you.

Individuals and organizations that you sell to will expect to get something of value for free. By something of value, I mean something that they can use. Your copy should cater to this expectation as directly (and ethically) as possible.

Putting Motivator 6 to Work in Your Correspondence

Step 1. Take two pieces of paper. On the first one write nonstop for a full ten minutes a list that includes every single service, study, evaluation, brainstorming session, survey, or other service you perform for your *prospects* that you currently do not charge for, because you're trying to get them to buy your stuff. Prepare yourself; it should be a long list. (If need be, get one of your peers or your sales manager to help out, or do this exercise at your next sales meeting.)

When you're done, take the other piece of paper and on it write nonstop for a full ten minutes every single service you perform for your *customers* that you don't currently charge them for. It should include your 24–7–365 help desk, your next-day service response, your conversations with application engineers, and so on. Whatever you do, write it all down. (As with the first exercise, get help if you need it.)

Don't cheat yourself by saying, "This or that isn't really important; our competition can do that, too." Write it down anyway. Chances are your competition isn't reading this book. Why? Because they're not as smart as you are.

Step 2. Now assign a dollar value to each and every one of the items on Sheet One and Sheet Two. Take the grand total and hold on to it. In just a minute, you'll learn how to take that list to the "correspondence bank."

Power-Writing Motivator 7: The Need to Work with an Authority in the Field

Becoming the authority figure you were meant to be is part of being a superior salesperson. Everyone (including your suspects and prospects) respects authority. They want to know that they're working with someone who is an authority on the topic at hand. After all, why else would they bother talking to you?

Nobody likes taking unnecessary risk. Nobody likes intentionally wasting time or making "unavoidable" mistakes. That's why people like to work with an authority in the field.

Putting Motivator 7 to Work in Your Correspondence

Do what it takes to be an authority figure:

- *Join and participate in every single association* that caters to the industry/niche or subgroups you sell to. That means go to the meetings, volunteer to help, join committees, and read their newsletters.
- *Subscribe to the periodicals* your suspects/prospects and customers subscribe to. Oh, I almost forgot. You must read whatever you subscribe to. And as you read, make sure you cut out any articles you think your current suspects/prospects and/or customers may be interested in. To make this a simple and enjoyable process, get yourself an old-fashioned file folder, and dedicate a tab to each of the prospects you're currently making an attempt to sell to. As you read the periodicals, tear out any article that addresses the needs of the prospect and make copies as required. Next time you call or visit that prospect, take the folder along with you—better yet, take the entire file with you wherever you go in your sales territory.
- *Be a sponge.* Whenever you're around any of your factory experts, make sure to take lots of notes and ask lots of questions. What questions should you ask? Well, for starters you should poll your prospects and ask them, "Could you do me a favor? I am getting ready to attend a conference call with our new product development manager. If you had one question to ask her, what would it be?" Write the question down, and when you get the answer, make sure you take it back to your prospect.

Take all of your newfound knowledge, and pepper your correspondence with the precise words, thoughts, phrases, and information that you learned. Integrate what you know with the information about your products, services, and solutions that's uniquely important to your particular reader.

Power-Writing Motivator 8: The Need for Certainty

Offer satisfaction beyond a guarantee.

How many times have you heard or seen words like "free trial period" and "satisfaction guaranteed"? Hundreds of times? Thousands of times? Hundreds of thousands of times? Now how many times have those words actually prompted you to take a second look at the offer in question? Hardly ever, right?

The key to this motivator is to offer not a guarantee, but a *satisfaction conviction*. A satisfaction conviction takes the idea of a guarantee to an entirely different level. Satisfaction conviction goes something like this:

Take your standard guarantee and make it so the people reading it will say to themselves, or out loud, "How can they do that?"

Now, I know that you're just a salesperson. And you most likely don't have the control and/or authority to go around changing your policies about guarantees. However, you do have the ability to present your guarantee in a way that will have the same effect as a satisfaction guarantee.

Putting Motivator 8 to Work in Your Correspondence

When was the last time you personally informed a prospect about your company's warranty and guarantee policies? Like most of the salespeople that I've met over the years, you probably never bother to read your firm's warranty and guarantee policy. Don't be like them. Read this stuff. Make it a part of your first pitch to your prospect.

> **Example**
>
> I recently went shopping for a washing machine; while in the store (a major supplier of appliances), I asked about an extended warranty. Gene, the salesperson, quickly informed me that if I purchased the extended package and my new machine broke down more than three times in the first year, the manufacturer would replace my machine with a new one. He also told me that for the duration of the extended warranty, the manufacturer would come and perform a preventative maintenance on my machine every three months for free. I decided to purchase the machine solely on the basis of its warranty program.

If you can build a similar appeal into your customized written correspondence, you should.

84

Power-Writing Motivator 9: The Need for Charisma

We're talking here about personality—but not yours. What's at issue is the personality of your product or service.

In order to present your product in an effective way to your prospects, you must be able to use the written word to explain in a compelling way the emotional impact of whatever it is you're selling. You must be able to communicate your product's essence—its nature, its flash—in a flash.

Putting Motivator 9 to Work in Your Correspondence

Before you move on to the next chapter, do the following exercise:

- Put your product in front of you. (If it's a D9 earthmoving bull-dozer, then a picture of it will do quite nicely.)
- Use your product. (If you don't know how to operate it, or if by operating it you would endanger your life or the lives of others, as with a portable emergency defibrillator, then picture a qualified individual using your product.)
- Now write 15 words or fewer to describe the nature of your product. What is its purpose in life? What emotional impact does it convey?
- Now condense your 15 words to seven.
- Now condense your seven words to three or four.

Here's what your list might look like:

- Learn how to make appointments with every organization that's predisposed to buying whatever you're selling. (15 words)
- Find the right place to sell quickly. (7 words)
- Stop cold calling, *forever!* (4 words)

Now you try it.

(15 words) _____

_____

_____

(7 words) _____

_____

(4 words) _____

_____

Power-Writing Motivator 10: The Need for Unique Connection

As a salesperson, it's your job to touch people in a special way.

I'm not talking about your handshake. I'm talking about developing a signature gift or strategy that accompanies every piece of initial correspondence you send to your prospects. For instance, you might think about passing along a personalized gift, or crafting a uniquely memorable closing salutation for your message.

Putting Motivator 10 to Work in Your Correspondence

What closing salutation do you use in your letters to new prospects? Perhaps it's *sincerely*. Did you know that this word just happens to be the single most popular word in written correspondence? The dictionary definition of sincerity includes the following phrase: "freedom from deceit."

As you'll recall, just a few paragraphs ago I suggested that you never write or say anything like "to be honest with you" or "to tell you the truth." Well, guess what? "Sincerely" falls into that category, too. Drop it. Instead, try a closing salutation that is something like this:

- To Greater Success!
- Make Today a Masterpiece!
- To Your Continued Success!
- Have a Blessed Day!

The only limit to your personal-touch strategy is your own imagination.

In the city of Atlanta, there's a shrewd salesperson who knows just how pressed her prospects are for time. She doesn't burden her most promising contacts with requests for in-person lunch meetings. Instead, she takes the time herself, and creates simple, healthy, tasty lunches that she nestles in an instantly recognizable red basket. Every Tuesday and Thursday, she makes three baskets and hand-delivers them to people to whom she's sent an "invitation" for a lunch date.

Talk about a memorable signature!

She manages to schedule—and conduct—three meetings on each of these days at: 11:45, 12:15, and 12:45.

Would you turn down such an offer? Would you ever forget the person who went to such lengths for you? When it comes time for her to ask for the business commitment, how do you think her prospects respond?

With the same canned "thanks but no thanks" brushoffs her less imaginative competitors receive? I think not.

One Big Idea

1. Don't move ahead until you've embraced all ten of the Power-Writing Motivators that you read about in this chapter.

Ok, now we're ready. Let's push on.

Notes

NO COLD-CALLING
PRINCIPLE 10

"Correspondence is to
selling as a salesperson
is to a presentation."

—E8486

CHAPTER TEN

Correspondence Boot Camp

T HIS IS A TRUE STORY.

Dave is a salesperson at the largest computer company in the world. He's responsible for millions of dollars of revenue generation each and every month. His product has lots of competition, his terri- tory is small, and his determination is big. He was skeptical about my No Cold-Calling model, but he decided to give it a try. This is what happened to Dave, according to Dave:

> Six weeks ago I sent 75 letters. About 50 were acknowledged during my first conversation, and I landed seven in-person appointments as a result.

By my calculations, the No Cold-Calling correspondence strategy you're about to learn got Dave an incredible 66 percent response rate and a 10 percent appointment ratio. What will *your* hit rate be? There's only one way to find out—keep reading and do the exercises in this chapter.

What Your Correspondence Has to Do

Your correspondence, at a bare minimum, must accomplish the following objectives if it is to make it possible for you to banish cold calling from your sales process:

- Introduce your ideas
- Pique the interest of the reader
- Establish your presence as an authority figure
- Create a sense of urgency

In other words, to do its job correctly, your correspondence needs to be a silent salesperson.

To compose correspondence that gets predisposed key players to buy from you, you must be willing to ask yourself a question that sounds simple, but really isn't: *What do your suspects and prospects want to read?*

That's the critical question in this chapter. As you look at the questions and exercises here and as you begin to formulate your answers, avoid answering as though you were answering them for yourself. Answer them from the point of view of your suspects and prospects. Once you have your answers, compare them to the answers that appear in the next chapter. If your responses are radically different, you will want to take a time out to get a reality check from no less than five of your territory's suspects and/or prospects. Sound fair?

Do not skip the activities in this chapter. Think of them as a boot camp. Completing every portion will help turn your correspondence into a lean, mean, selling machine. Just like you.

Everywhere you see the word *prospect*, add the words *that fit my TIP*. If you don't know what a TIP is, stop reading right now, and go back to page 1 of this book.

Four Indisputable Laws of No Cold-Calling Written Correspondence

- *Law 1.* Your correspondence must be easily scanned before it is read, and it must be a quick read.

90

- *Law 2.* Your correspondence must be relevant to current situations and circumstances (problems and opportunities) for which the reader wants some type of resolution.
- *Law 3.* Your correspondence must be written so the reader can easily understand it and take action.
- *Law 4.* Your correspondence must be easily forwarded to someone other than the recipient or, if need be, archived for easy retrieval at a later date and time.

Ready, set, GO.

The Nine Elements of Correspondence

There are nine elements of the correspondence that you'll be creating that are quite easy to get your arms around. The tenth element deals with the way you'll be delivering your correspondence, and that's where the rubber is going to hit the road. This could very well be the most exciting road trip in your sales career. Dump any old baggage. You won't be needing it from this point forward.

Element 1: The Words We Use

Remember that Approvers love benefits, Decision Makers lean toward advantages, Influencers understand features, and Recommenders will always embrace functions. In short, don't lose sight of your audience. Make sure that you use words and/or phrases that are of interest to the recipient of your correspondence.

Let's do an exercise together. I'll use the example of a salesperson selling pharmaceuticals to the health-care industry, and in the spaces provided, you create statements using whatever it is that you sell.

Benefit Statements

Key words: Results, value, lasting, goals, plans, objectives, initiatives, strategies, enhancing, exceeding, achieving, overachieving, time.

Statement: "Two of the top 20 hospitals in San Diego County are exceeding their strategic goals of enhancing patient care while at the same time cutting costs. As a result, their patients receive more value from the doctors during each visit."

Write your statement here: _____

_____

_____

_____

Advantage Statements

Key words: edge, tailor, customize, tactical, solution, increase, decrease, time.

Statement: "We can tailor each of our solutions to give your department the edge in increasing key employee efficiency while at the same time further decreasing costs."

Write your statement here: _____

_____

_____

_____

Feature Statements

Key words: performance, form, fit, capabilities, specifications, precise, precision, any product name and/or number, any mention of a higher authority/compliance/institution.

Statement: "Our extended shelf life Aplex PH delivers the precise dosage within specifications required by the FDA."

Write your statement here: _____

_____

_____

_____

Function Statements

Key words: use, proper, procedure, follow, simple, easy.

Statement: "When mixing the Aplex PH into other meds, the procedure is simple, straightforward, and safeguarded by its color-coded banding."

Write your statement here: _____

_____

_____

_____

Never Mix and Match!

Write for one—and only one—of the four target audiences. Do not break this rule under any circumstances!

Imagine a statement that reads like this:

> *Two of the top 20 hospitals in San Diego County are exceeding their strategic goals of enhancing patient care while at the same time cutting costs. As a result, their patients receive more value from the doctors during each visit.*

This statement is benefit-centric and intended for the Approver's eyes. But what if you sent it to an Influencer? Here's the internal monologue that would result:

> *I don't give a hoot about exceeding strategic goals. I need something to help fill prescriptions quickly, and accurately, while also maintaining compliance with the FDA. Who writes this junk anyway?*

Or try this one on for size:

> *Our Aplex PH delivers the precise dosage within specifications required by the FDA.*

Reading this, an Approver will think, or perhaps scream:

> *Precise dosage my *&%#! That's why I have 35 pharmacies. Can't anyone tell me anything I don't already know about how to remedy rising costs and declining patient care?*

Find out as much as you can about the organization ahead of time. Whenever possible, start high with the Approvers. And target your message carefully to your reader's role.

Element 2: Your Headline

Just like a newspaper or magazine article, each piece of correspondence you create must have an attention-getting headline.

On average, people decide within about eight seconds whether or not to continue reading just about anything you put in front of them. Your headline should blast the horn for and about actual events and/or results, not hypothetical situations. Your headline should also:

1. not exceed 30 words in length
2. address this suspect/prospect's role and interest in a very direct way

Let's say you're selling laptop computers to large corporations that have salespeople who need to communicate with their office while they're on the road. Here's an example of how your headline statement might evolve.

Influencer Headline

Micro Plasma display technology is reliable, readable, and now available on all of our high-speed satellite laptop connectivity devices.

Recommender Headline

While our satellite link keeps you connected to your home office, you can work faster—not harder—with a keyboard and display that's easy for you to see and read in direct sunlight.

Decision Maker Headline

Salespeople can increase the time they spend in front of their prospects and customers by as much as 50 percent—within two months of using our solutions.

Approver Headline

Increase marketplace mindshare by as much as 30 to 50 percent while lowering cost of sales—in just two months.

Now Write Your Own Headlines

Pull out the Product Value Inventory you did in Chapter Four. Using it as a working document, take the time to create your own headlines. Remember, you'll need one for the Recommender, Influencer, Decision Maker, and Approver of your sale.

Influencer: _____

_____

_____

_____

Recommender: _____

_____

_____

_____

Decision Maker: _____

_____

_____

_____

Approver: _____

_____

_____

_____

Element 3: The First Sentence of Each Paragraph

What you write (or don't write) in the first sentence of a paragraph will greatly impact your reader's desire to read the second sentence. Therefore, the goal of the first sentence is:

> Get the reader to read the second sentence.

How to get 'em to the second sentence? Keep it short.

Think about the articles you read in a magazine or newspaper. The first sentence in a paragraph is usually the shortest one. It plants the seed and gets the reader to want to read more.

Here are examples of good, crisp opening sentences for a paragraph:

1. Make your job easier and more fun.   _____
2. Compliance will keep the feds off your back. _____
3. Surpass required specifications.   _____
4. Shorten time to revenue.   _____

Take a moment, and look at the four examples above. Write on the line provided which one of our players—Approver, Decision Maker,

Influencer, or Recommender—would respond favorably to each first sentence.

If your answer to the mini-quiz above was anything but (a) Recommender, (b) Approver, (c) Influencer, and (d) Decision Maker, stop reading this book right now, and take one of two actions:

1. Ask yourself why you have A.D.D.
2. Go back to the beginning of Chapter Seven and reread it.

For the first sentence, consider using larger type size than the second sentence and/or bold typeface and/or italicized print.

Consider the following examples:

Compliance will keep the feds off your back. We're working for 75 other CEOs in the health-care industry to ensure the privacy and safety of their corporate records.

Or:

Compliance will keep the feds off your back. We're working for 75 other CEOs in the health-care industry to ensure the privacy and safety of their corporate records.

Or:

Compliance will keep the feds off your back. We're working for 75 other CEOs in the health care industry to ensure the privacy and safety of their corporate records.

Or:

Compliance will keep the feds off your back. We're working for 75 other CEOs in the health-care industry to ensure the privacy and safety of their corporate records.

Element 4: The Job of the Second Sentence

Let me ask you: What do you think the job of the second sentence is? That's exactly right. To get the reader to dive headfirst into the third sentence.

If you're asking when does this stop, the answer is not until you're sure you've got the reader hooked. And how do you get the reader hooked? You do so by continuing to pique the reader's interest by pitching a benefit, advantage, feature, or function (depending upon whom you're writing to).

Now you write it. Grab a big piece of paper and create a first and second sentence for an Approver, Decision Maker, Influencer, and Recommender prospect in your territory. In other words, when you're done, you'll have four sets of first and second sentences.

Go ahead. I'll wait right here for you.

Element 5: Your First Paragraph

No surprises here. The job of your first paragraph is to carry the entire theme of the headline into the body of the letter—and keep the reader's interest. It's best to make the following points in your first paragraph:

1. Establish your credibility by posing a profound relevant question.
2. Make a relevant statement from a creditable source.
3. Make sure you address the concerns of your reader—and nobody else. (Remember to keep your focus on the Approver, Decision Maker, Influencer, or Recommender.)
4. Segue into the next element of your correspondence.

Here are some examples:

Approver: During the last seven years, we have worked with 80 organizations in the manufacturing industry, including ABC, XYZ, and BBB. Collectively, we've been able to increase revenues and efficiencies while at the same time providing annuities that continue to increase shareholder value every month.

Decision Maker: The above results are common for our business partners to achieve. Team-member resources once unintentionally wasted on inefficiencies are now channeled to generate on-time and under-budget results.

Influencer: While you consider and validate the contents of this document, our technology department scientists are making sure that we offer the most tested, proven products for your evaluation.

Recommender: We are pleased to present the following timesaving ideas for your use in creating your sales reports faster and with greater accuracy. And no matter where you happen to be, at your convenience.

Now, write your first paragraph. This may seem like a lot of work. But let me ask you this: Does it beat making cold calls?

Thought so. Let's keep going. Take a moment, flip that piece of paper over, and create a first paragraph for your correspondence similar to the ones you just read, but make them yours. No shortcuts. Do your work.

Element 6: Create Your Selling Environment

What's your best selling environment? In other words, do you sell best in person while at the prospect's office, during a demo of your products at your facility, on a golf course, or during a business lunch? How about over the telephone? As you ponder that question, let me suggest that the correspondence you send to your prospects must create a selling environment and by doing so, you'll begin your sales process before you even talk to your prospect.

Charts and Graphs

It's often said that a picture speaks a thousand words. Well, guess what? So does a pie chart, or a bar graph. You can also use a comparison chart or any chart that shows a situation that you can solve. Your chart can depict what was taking place before and after your products, services, and solutions were put in place.

Whenever you use a chart or graph, the reader can quickly see what results are possible. It's also easy for readers to compare their situation to what the possibilities are.

The Silver Bullet

If you can't create your selling environment with a chart of some sort, you can use brief statements of your ability articulated in the form of bullets. They must address by all means the most important results—benefits for Approvers, advantages for Decision Makers, features for Influencers, and functions for Recommenders—that your product, service, or solution can provide. They are short, to the point, and in simple language. Think of them as ammo.

Here are some examples.

Approver Ammo
- In the words of [John Brown], President of [ABC], "an overwhelming increase in the efficiency and positive attitude of our support staff."

- Obtain [greater market share] by creating more new business with prospects—in some cases, [70 percent] more.
- [Increase customer retention] and eliminate erosion of [hard-earned market share]. An average of [13 percent increase in quarterly revenues].
- [Reduced production expense, with time savings] ranging from [one] to [six] months, and no compromises on [quality].

Decision-Maker Ammo
- Shorten the [launch window] for the new products by an average of [one full month].
- Decrease departmental [quality complaints] from consumers by an average of [24 percent] within [two months].
- Reduce cost of administration by eliminating unnecessary items that must be ordered, stored, and distributed to and from your knowledge-based workers.
- Use our experienced team of consultants at no cost. Our account teams are the best trained in the [life sciences] industry, and tailor simple but effective solutions to your unique needs.

Influencer Ammo
- Compress the length of time needed to evaluate and prioritize projects through the effectiveness of our program generator.
- Eliminate errors in programming code.
- Exert greater control over internal communications with all local and remote team members.
- Reduce costs of all consultant-driven outsourced projects.

Recommender Ammo
- Unparalleled customer service. [John Brown] at [Rogers & Rogers Auto-Port] has already experienced how responsive and knowledgeable our help desk personnel are, with wait times less than two minutes.
- Unlimited onsite training is available at your convenience 24–7–365.
- Save time and enjoy your work environment with our five-second guarantee for locating any document on your computer network.

Now create a few silver bullets of your own. You knew I was going to ask you to do this. Stop whining. Grab another piece of paper and create at least three silver bullets for your Approver, Decision Maker, Influencer, and Recommender.

Hint: Use the Product Value Inventory you created in Chapter Four.

Element 7: Your Closing Sentences

The main purpose and point in closing your correspondence is to introduce an element of uncertainty and doubt about whether or not you could reproduce your success with this organization.

You want the reader of your masterpiece to say out loud, "Why not? Why couldn't we do something similar or even better?"

Don't worry. This approach will not create doubt in your prospect's mind about your ability or your product, service, or solution. It will add a dose of reality to all of the prior claims in your correspondence. That wins you points in the credibility department.

Approver Examples

- Could your company realize similar or even more substantial benefits? Frankly, at this point it's too early to tell. But I would welcome the opportunity to learn more about your unique business needs and take the first steps to finding out.
- We would like your valued opinion on some of our growth management solutions and if they could possibly work for you in [year].
- Whether your company can achieve these results is difficult to tell. But one part is certain: you are the only person who can take the action necessary to help us quickly determine what the possibilities are.

Decision Maker Examples

- You know your department better than anyone. Would you welcome an effort to uncover these potential savings? Together we can quickly determine what, if any, the possibilities are.
- Because both of our companies are committed to [Total Quality Management Programs], it would be interesting to get together to see if we can use these principles to achieve similar or even greater savings in your area of profit-and-loss responsibility.

100

- Do these results fit into your business plans for the balance of [this year]? You may be asking yourself, "Can these people actually deliver similar or greater results?" The fact is, we don't know. However, with your help we can quickly find out.

Influencer Examples

- [Your company name] has brought these, as well as many other technologies, to [14,000] companies across [this prospect's industry]. However, your requirements are unique. Would you like to explore the possibilities by the end of this week?
- You are the person who has the knowledge to evaluate our ideas. We stand ready to make your evaluation complete and accurate in a time frame that would help your current project workload and budget.
- Can your department achieve similar or greater results? Quite honestly, I'm not sure. But if it is feasible, you are the individual who can quickly start the process and evaluate what the possibilities are.

Recommender Examples

- We would like your valued opinion on some of our ideas and how they might work for you and your [school district].
- With your help we could find out if our [your product name goes here] could add value to your day-to-day work flow and make your job easier.
- Not all these results can be easily duplicated. The real question becomes: "Can we deliver greater results to your day-to-day tasks? You are the person who can provide a reality check and see if it can work for you."

Element 8: Your Call to Action

You must always give the reader a choice of different ways that you or they can take action at or near the end of the correspondence. There are three different ways to do this:

1. You state a day, date, and time that you're going to call them.
2. You give them two choices of days, dates, and times that they can call you.

3. You provide them with a fax-back form with questions that they must answer before either of the aforementioned takes place.

Notice that you shouldn't use any of the following options as part of your call to action:

1. A date for a face-to-face meeting, such as:

   "I would like to set up a meeting so I can show you the many ways that our 'Cure-all' industrial cleaner can save your janitorial staff time and money."

2. A vague offer for the reader to call you with any questions, such as:

   "If you have any questions, call me at your convenience."

3. An offer for the reader to ask for additional information, such as:

   "If you would like any further information, feel free to call me anytime."

4. A nebulous offer to contact them, such as:

   "I'll call you sometime next week to set up an appointment."

These approaches turn the prospect off. Skip 'em.

Element 9: Your Closing Salutation

Not too long ago I received a correspondence from a high-net-worth financial planner here in San Diego. The letter was printed on elegant paper, and it addressed several of my areas of interest. It also stated that this firm paid close attention to all of the many critical details that a professional financial planner takes pride in doing for select clientele.

All very impressive. However, I was shocked to see that the sender had neglected to sign the letter.

Your signature, and the salutation that precedes it, is more or less your personal brand. It leaves a lasting impression. (And so does the absent-mindedness evident in botching it.) Therefore, we must be sure that it's the best it can possibly be.

Here are some suggestions.

Don't:

- close your correspondence with "Sincerely" or anything similar to it.
- use any nicknames, such as Clarence "Butch" Dumstuff.

- put your closing salutation on the left-hand margin.
- forget to sign your name.

Do:

- put in your entire name.
- put your title under your name.
- put your company name under your title (if it's nowhere else in your correspondence).
- put your telephone number under your title. (Don't use your cell-phone number.)

The actual words of your closing salutation should be as original and unique as your handshake. And just like your handshake, it matches the person you are shaking hands with. Here are some examples of my closing salutations. I offer these only as suggestions. Of course, you'll have to do some creative soul-searching to develop your own.

Approver

- To your continued success.
- Make today a masterpiece.

Decision Maker

- Looking forward to being part of your team.
- To a more predictable future.

Influencer

- Have a productive day.
- Looking forward to your evaluation.

Recommender

- Thanks in advance for your interest.
- Looking forward to meeting you.

Write your own salutations for each of the four groups in the space below:

Approver: _____

_____

Decision Maker: _____

Influencer: _____

Recommender: _____

Whew. You really did all that stuff, right? Good. Now that you've got the nine critical elements of your correspondence down, let's push on to the next chapter. There you'll learn how to launch the wave of correspondence that will support the No Cold-Calling sales model.

Five Big Ideas

1. Your correspondence must be easily scanned before it's read, and it must be a quick read.

2. Your correspondence must be relevant to current situations and circumstances (problems and opportunities) that the reader wants some type of resolution for.

3. Your correspondence must be written so the reader can easily understand it and take action.

4. Your correspondence must be easily forwarded to someone other than the recipient or, if need be, archived for easy retrieval at a later date and time.

5. Master the critical correspondence elements covered in this chapter.

Don't forget to go to www.stopcoldcalling.info for additional for-fee information. Click on "Chapter Ten: Online Assets."

Notes

NO COLD-CALLING
PRINCIPLE 11

"Anticipation creates sales."

—E8486

CHAPTER ELEVEN

The Wave

C AUTION: IF YOU HAVEN'T READ, UNDERSTOOD, *AND COMPLETED* ALL OF THE exercises in the prior chapters, what you're about to read will do you no good. Specifically, for anyone who may have imagined that it's possible to get the benefits of this portion of the book without first completing the boot-camp instructions laid out in Chapter Nine and the information in Chapter Ten, I have a simple message: Think again, Private.

Do not proceed to the material in this chapter unless you have finished *all* the material in the previous chapters.

That's an order!

What's That Rumbling Sound?

I am a far cry from being a sports fan. I don't follow any spectator sport. But I have, on my occasional visits to the local ballpark, witnessed the effects of the wave. It starts in some isolated portion of the stadium. You can barely see it. It's small at first. And then it quickly builds momentum. By the time it hits your corner of the bleachers, you're swept up in it. Without so much as a second thought, you throw your arms up and jump into the air along with the thousands of other crazies at the stadium. You scream at the top of your lungs and go along with the crowd as the rush of energy makes its way across the stands.

> A good friend of mine, an expert car salesperson, has on more than one occasion tossed up a handful of his business cards with a handwritten note on the back: "I'll pay you $100 if you or anyone you know buys a car from me." This activity has brought him more than one new customer, while giving a new meaning to a typical ballpark wave.

This is the type of excitement your correspondence wave will build within your suspect's and prospect's world. By the time you pick up the telephone or visit in person, your contact will be ready, willing, and available to speak with you.

Sound far-fetched? Read on.

How It Will Happen?

A prospect of yours (one who works at a company that fits your TIP to a T) is sitting at her desk at about 11:00 A.M. on a Tuesday morning. She's an Approver. You figured that much out by checking her company's Web site.

Your Approver is looking at a stack of incoming mail. In that pile, she spots a uniquely strange, brightly-colored postcard. Curious, she grabs for it, puts it right at the top of the pile, and reads its 26-word message:

> *Your e-mail contains an idea from our CEO.*
> *The title is "My Call on Thursday, May 14, at 9:00 A.M."*
> *We invite you to read it!*

What's going to happen?

Take a wild guess.

Your Approver's behavior is, I guarantee you, going to be utterly predictable. She will wake up her dormant computer screen and check her e-mail for the titled message.

But it's not going to be there. Not yet anyway.

So she will leave the postcard out and put it close to her keyboard—or perhaps make a mental note or quickly key into her PDA *"Look for e-mail from CEO re: 5/14."*

Later that day, the Approver scans her e-mail again. And then she sees it. "My Call on Thursday, May 14, at 9:00 A.M." And bless her heart, she reads every single word of it.

The rest of the message reads. . . Naaah. Let's wait. I'll show it to you later.

Another Way It Might Happen

A prospect of yours (who happens to work at an organization that fits your TIP to a T) is sitting at his desk on a Monday morning. He's a Decision Maker. You were able to figure that much out by talking to one of your suppliers, who has this company as a customer. (Oh, the power of networking.)

The Decision Maker is looking at a stack of incoming mail at about 8:00 A.M. on a Wednesday morning. (It's a big company, and the mailroom doesn't sort and deliver everything that came in the previous day until first thing the next morning.)

There, sticking out of the pile by its crimson edge, is a bright red postcard.

Your Decision Maker pulls it out and reads its 30-word message:

> *A fax has been sent to you from our*
> *Marketing Line-of-Business Executive*
> *titled "My Call on Thursday, May 14, at 10:00 A.M."*
> *We invite you to read it.*

What's going to happen?

Take a wild guess.

Your Decision Maker's behavior is, I guarantee you, going to be utterly predictable. He will walk over to the fax machine and check for the message.

109

But it's not going to be there. Not yet anyway.

So he will take the postcard, put it on his desk (not in the round file), and make a mental note to keep on the lookout for it. Later that day, he will make a point of checking the fax machine—and there it is: "My Call on Thursday, May 14, at 10:00 A.M." He reads it carefully as he walks back to his office.

It says. . . . Well, I'll get to that later.

Yet Another Way It Might Happen

A prospect of yours (who happens to work at an organization that fits your TIP to a T) is sitting at her desk on a Thursday morning. She is an Influencer. You figured that much out by reading an e-mail she posted on a newsgroup you subscribe to.

She is sitting at her desk, looking at a stack of incoming mail. The stack includes trade rags and other technical documents. She's got a lot of work to do, so she figures everything in the stack can probably wait. Just before she turns to look at a schematic for her most recent project, though, she sees an incoming fax message sitting in a different pile.

It's addressed to her.

Nobody, but nobody, faxes anything to this lady. She lives, breathes, and eats e-mail.

This is weird.

She thinks to herself, "Hmm, I haven't received a fax in ages. What's this about?" She grabs it and reads its 28-word message:

> *Your e-mail contains a presentation from our*
> *Head Fiber Optics Scientist.*
> *The title is "My Call on Thursday, May 14, at 1:00 P.M."*
> *We invite you to read it.*

What's going to happen?

Take a wild guess.

Your Influencer's behavior is, I guarantee you, going to be utterly predictable. She will click her e-mail for the titled e-presentation.

But it's not going to be there. Not yet anyway.

So she will pull out her PDA and point-and-click herself an entry for later that day, in an available slot, of course: "11:15—check for e/p f.o."

110

At precisely 11:15 A.M. a little alarm will go off on the Influencer's hip holster. She'll retrieve her PDA, head for her desk, scan her e-mail, and then she'll see it.

"My Call on Thursday, May 14, at 1:00 P.M."

She'll click on it and read the following. . . I'll get to that right now.

Creating a Selling Environment

In this chapter I'll discuss many different, different ways for you to create a selling environment that will support your No Cold-Calling sales model. Just a word of caution before we get started: Throw away words and phrases like "I can't," "It won't," "don't," "never," "always," "why bother," "what for," and any other such self-limiting, creativity-killing phrases. You won't be needing them, not ever again.

One Common Theme

Not long ago, during my radio talk-show, "Selling Across America," a caller asked me for one tip that would make his success in sales certain. Here's the answer I gave him:

Perform common sales work in an uncommon way.

If you are serious about performing common sales work in an uncommon way, you must make sure your sales message (no matter how you choose to deliver it) becomes truly memorable. This means creating a new kind of selling environment.

Creating a No Cold-Calling selling environment can be done by using one of the following delivery modes.

First-Class Mail

These days, e-mail is so popular that first-class mail is almost forgotten in some circles. So send a letter. That will stand out from all the rest.

I'm not talking about any letter. I'm talking about one that looks like Figure 11.1 on page 112.

Here's How You'll Send It

In a *plain white* envelope, *without* your company logo on it.

FIGURE 11.1: Sample Correspondence

> *A top-ten advertising firm increased net working capital by $345,000 while improving office efficiency by 12% in just three months. These are proven results based upon our repeatable process.*

May 14, 2004

Mr. Bigshot
President

Dear Mr. Bigshot,

During the past seven years, we have worked with 30 organizations in the advertising industry, including three of the top-ten agencies. Collectively, we've been able to increase revenues and efficiencies while at the same time providing ways to increase shareholder value.

Are any of the following achievements on your list of goals, plans, or objectives for the balance of this calendar year? If so, the good news is that we have created a proven, repeatable process that we guarantee to deliver results such as:

- *Expansion of national account volume* by as much as 250 percent, by adapting the precise sales and operations methodology these larger customers demand as a condition of doing business.
- *Reducing time to resolve unpaid invoices* from as long as five months to as short as five seconds! Imagine the impact to top, middle, and bottom lines. Resolving these issues also improves customer retention by as much as 12 percent—an unbeatable combination!
- *Expense reduction by as much as* $72,000 *monthly*, without compromising the level of services or associated assets.

Mr. Bigshot, it's obvious you know your organization better than anyone does. But what may not be so obvious is how our ideas and commitments to your success could help you realize similar or even greater results before the end of this calendar year.

If you would like to take the first step, our complete team of experts can quickly determine each and every possibility.

Regards,

Will Prosper

Will Prosper
800-777-8486

P.S. I will call your office on Thursday, May 19, at 10:00 A.M. If this is an inconvenient time, please have Tommie inform me as to when I should place the call.

Yep. No logo. No razzmatazz. Use your own name and your company's address. Drop the suite number. Along the bottom of the envelope, on the flap side write this:

Contains information for our telephone call
on Thursday, May 14, at 10:00 A.M.

Want to make it even more powerful? Sure you do. So, write:

Miki, this contains information for Ms. Bigtime's call
on Thursday, May 14, at 10:00 A.M.

Of course, this only works for the Approver and/or Decision Maker who happens to have a secretary or assistant; that would be Miki, of course.

Postcards

One of the most forgotten, powerful tools in sales correspondence available today is a simple postcard with no more than 30 words on it. Forget about printing them, forget about putting postage on them, forget about sorting them, and forget about having to design them. Just go to: www.USPS.com—that stands for United States Postal Service, of course. Click on: "Direct Mail Services." Then click on: "Premium Postcards." Bingo! You've landed in the point-and-click, create-my-best-ever-postcard world. The postal service will help you design your card, and it'll print it out and mail it that same day (first-class mail) for about $.37 each, no matter how many or how few you send.

This is probably the best implementation of just-in-time print marketing I've ever seen.

Here are some examples of what you can use a postcard for:

- Set a time for your first telephone call.
- Alert your prospect that an e-mail is on its way.
- Alert your prospect that an e-presentation is on its way.
- Alert your prospect that you'll be stopping in to see him or her at a certain day, date, and time.
- Invite your suspects, prospects, and/or customers to a telephone seminar (more on this later).

Faxing

Yep, faxes can work wonders—as supporting players, anyway. But don't use your standard, run-of-the-mill company-issue cover sheet. You know, the one that has your logo proudly displayed at the top of it, the one that has your 800 numbers and your address on it. Instead, take a completely different approach.

- Use an oversized 8½ x 11-size copy of the postcard you sent (see above).
- Use an 8½ x 11-size copy of the envelope that you sent your letter in.
- Use an 8½ x 11-size copy of the typical "While You Were Out" slip.

At the end of this chapter you'll be invited to go to an online learning center where you'll find examples of all of this wonderful stuff.

Always use a fax message to call attention to another message.

Always keep your fax message to two pages maximum, including whatever cover sheet you may eventually use (see below). No exceptions.

Get even more creative when contacting your four groups.

Faxing the Approver: Get a copy of her or his annual report. Take the front page, and use it as your cover sheet.

Here are some ideas for what you should write on that unorthodox cover page:

- *An interesting idea follows to assist you in [over-accomplishing your mission]. See page 2.*
- *See page 2 for our idea to [shorten time to revenue].* NOTE: What you'll put in the brackets is the most talked-about initiative that you read about in his or her annual report, or something that you know he or she is interested in just by the nature of the company's industry.
- *We have an early-adopter idea for your consideration. See page 2.*

Faxing the Decision Maker: You'll recall that the job of the typical Decision Maker is to say "yes," so let's make it easy for her or him to do just that. Try this on your cover page:

- *See page 2 for the first of three steps to ensure [under-budget/over-plan] performance for your entire [sales team].*
- *[Increase knowledge-based worker effectiveness while lowering expenses]. See page 2.*
- *A special message from our [Sales-Line-of-Business-Executive, Jere Calmes] on page 2.* (Of course, you'll pick the line of business that aligns perfectly with this Decision Maker's title.)

Faxing the Influencer. Get an 8½ x 11 high-resolution, black-and-white copy of your latest and greatest product's data sheet. Here's the sort of thing you should write on it:

- *We would love to get your opinion on our [compliance performance].*
- *Our design engineer wants your opinions.*
- *Seats still available at our design symposium. Details follow.*

Faxing the Recommender. Get an 8½ x 11 "teamwork" or other success-oriented, inspirational black-and-white, high-resolution image, and write on it:

- *Looking for an easier way to [get reports completed while having fun]? Take a look at sheet 2.*
- *Interested in learning new ways to [get more unpleasant tasks done faster]? Look at what follows.*
- *Free Trial Offer. [Learn how to use your computer.] See page 2.*

E-Mail

This is one overused, hypersensitive, regulated, spam-ulated communication mode. Let's face it: e-mail has been beaten into the ground. Even so, we can't seem to live without it. So here are some tips:

- Give the viewer an audio option.
- Give the viewer a link to go to a particular page on your company Web site. (Duh.)
- Give the viewer a link to your private/personal Web site. (Hmm. Not so duh.)
- Make sure you use a compelling topic or subject line. (My favorite is: "Our Call on Thursday, May 14, at 10:00 A.M.")

Warning: In all such appeals, make sure you take into account any time zone difference that may exist between you and your prospect. (It only takes one stupid mistake to ram your credibility into the highway divider.)

115

Equally Important Warning: Make sure you pick a date and a time that's sensitive to your prospect's business environment. For example, you may want to avoid the end of the month if your prospect is in the business of manufacturing anything.

E-Presentations

It's amazing how many tools are available in this area that aren't being used by salespeople. You can see two of my favorites by going to Chapter Eleven: Online Assets at www.stopcoldcalling.info. Both are extremely easy to use and will merge your voice (or the voice of your CEO, head of your product development team, or a satisfied customer) and your Microsoft PowerPoint slides. Before you go plunging your browser, though, consider the following points:

- Any e-presentation you create and send must be as short as possible.
- Never exceed three slides per presentation.
- Never have more than ten words on each slide.
- Never speak for more than ten seconds per slide.

The Blended Approach

In picking communication modes, everyone has a tendency to migrate toward what they feel most comfortable with. However, your comfort zone isn't what's important here. What is at stake is finding out what your prospects will be open to and what puts your products, services, and solutions in the best possible light before you even pick up the phone.

Here are some suggestions of how to mix the approaches that I have used over the years to create a wave of my own.

Combo 1

- Send a first-class letter.
- Pick up the telephone and call, or
- Make an in-person appearance.

Combo 2

- Send a postcard.
- Send an e-mail.
- Pick up the phone and call.

Combo 3

- Send a postcard.
- Send a unique, personalized e-presentation.
- Pick up the telephone and call, or
- Make an in-person appearance.

Combo 4

- Pick up the telephone and call (talk live or leave a voice mail message).
- Send a unique, personalized e-presentation.

Combo 5

- Send a fax.
- Send a unique, personalized e-presentation.
- Pick up the telephone and call.

My guess is it's going to take a bit of trial and error on your part to figure out what works best for you. What I can give you is a guarantee that you won't be in violation of any government regulation by using any one of the five combinations. (This is assuming, of course, that you *do not* send mass e-mails to people you don't know. *Do* reach out as one professional to another with a unique e-mail message; *do* include your physical address in any e-mail message; and *do* maintain an accurate drop list of people who ask not to receive further messages from you.) And make sure that in every single case the prospect you're sending your wave to fits your TIP to a T.

What I can't give you is a guarantee that you won't tick anyone off. The fact of the matter is, with everything that everyone has going on these days, it's hard to predict how anyone will react to your messages until you take action. If you do push someone's irritation button, you can use the words that I've used over the years and personally found to be quite effective:

I am very sorry.

What's Next?

Because each of my combinations ends up in either a telephone call or an in-person interaction, let's move on to the next chapter, one of my personal favorites: The contact sport of using the telephone.

One Big Idea

1. Perform common sales work in an uncommon way.

Don't forget to go to www.stopcoldcalling.info for additional for-fee information. Click on "Chapter Eleven: Online Assets."

Notes

NO COLD-CALLING
PRINCIPLE 12

"Icebreakers are for ships—
not salespeople."

—E8486

Old Dog, New Dog

B Y MY CALCULATIONS, 96 MILLION COLD-CALL ATTEMPTS ARE MADE EACH AND
every business day in the United States.

Unfortunately, the primary economic beneficiary of all this cold
calling activity is the phone company.

Just in case you suspect me of pulling my numbers out of my pro-
boscis (I'll wait here while you go and look that up. But trust me, it's perfectly safe), here's how I got that 96 million figure.

- The last U.S. Census showed that more than 16 million American
  men and women are actively engaged in professional selling.
- Somewhere around 40 percent of these folks are in retail sales posi-
  tions that don't require them to make cold calls.
- That leaves 9.6 million dialers on the phone most every day, making their telephone approach to unsuspecting strangers.

- Typically, these hunters will make anywhere between 0 and 50 dials each day in an attempt to give their sales pitch and/or set appointments for themselves or for an outside sales rep.
- Not everyone in sales dials the phone 50 times a day. Let's assume 20 percent of the salespeople in America hunt for new business at this calling level. Therefore we can estimate that, at a minimum,

$$1,920,000 \text{ (salespeople)} \times 50 \text{ (call attempts per business day)}$$
$$= 96,000,000.$$

I have to own up here. In years past, I myself made thousands of cold calls, thereby contributing to the grand total of madness and futility. But, as you'll recall from the subtitle of this wonderful book, I have reformed.

What's interesting is that many of my calls worked. However, *most of them didn't.*

I'm living proof that an old dog really can master some pretty interesting new tricks. If sales is a numbers game (and I believe it is), then this is the chapter where you learn to stack the odds in your favor, just as I did and continue to do.

The Old-Dog Calling Model

Here's the way I used to make cold calls, and the way just about everyone makes them today.

Salesperson: "Good morning, how are you today? Have I caught you at a good time? Okay, well, my name is Ima Looser, and I work for Yadayada Communications. We've got the fastest DSL wireless connection in the world, and I'd like to tell you how we can save you time and money. Is that of interest to you?"

Prospect: "No." (Click. Dial tone.)

or

Salesperson: "Hello, Mr. (little pause) Parianellalalleo, my name is Will Perish, and the purpose of my call today is to tell you about our newest offer in our line of office copiers. Are you the person who makes the decisions on office equipment? Good, I can show you how to consolidate your equipment population while at the same time taking advantage of our month-end special on rental equipment.

Would it be better if I came by today at, oh, let's say 2:00, or would tomorrow at 10:30 be better?"

Prospect: "I've got all the copiers I need." (Click. Dial tone.)

or

Salesperson: "Good day, sir. And how are *you* doing today? Great. This is Justin Tyme with Blahblah Recovery Systems. If you're like the other entrepreneurs we serve in the greater Hermosa Beach area, you'll love our newest guaranteed collection service. How much bad debt are you currently carrying?"

Prospect: "That's none of your business. Take a hike." (Click. Dial tone.)

Is It Any Wonder the People We Talk to Are Hostile?

That's the old way of calling. It shouldn't surprise us if most (or all) of those 50 strangers we reach out to every day say rude things or hang up on us.

It's time to teach the old dog some new tricks. Actually, it may be time to turn the entire old dog into a whole new dog.

So do something different. Throw away all of those old calling habits that have given the profession of sales a bad name. Adopt a telephone and in-person approach that will allow the prospect to lean into you and your approach, not push you away. (Remember, a prospect is someone, or a bunch of someones, who fits your TIP to a T.)

From this point on, I'm assuming:

1. You've decided to use the telephone to hold your first conversation with a prospect as a follow-up call on a written communication of some kind.
2. Your ultimate goal is to get an in-person appointment with someone (Approver, Decision Maker, Influencer, and/or Recommender) in your territory.
3. Steps 1 and 2 above are going to follow your wave (see Chapter Eleven).

In other words, the goal of this call (whether you expect it, don't expect it, or once expected it and have forgotten about it) is not to close the sale, but rather to get someone to commit a particular chunk of his or her schedule to a face-to-face meeting or telephone conversation with you.

To the extent that your call helps you accomplish these goals, it's working for you.

To the extent that it doesn't help you accomplish these things, it's not working.

Pretty simple, right?

By the way, what you're about to learn can (and should) be applied to situations where you're meeting in person, for the first time, with an important contact who's never had any significant interaction with you. Remember, in such a situation, you're not out to sell. You're out to win attention and interest and to get your prospect to commit to taking the next step, whatever that might be.

What's That Burning Smell?

When I think of the typical salesperson approaching a prospect for the first time, I think of the salesperson as a piece of bread and the conversation as a hyperactive toaster oven. If things don't go right in the first few seconds—toast, well done.

Take another look at those old-dog calls I outlined for you. What's insane about these scripts is that they virtually guarantee that the first few seconds of the conversation will go poorly.

Six Steps of a Highly Successful Initial Call

There are six steps to a successful first interaction with any prospect.

1. Make a great first impression.
2. Make whatever you say sound conversational.
3. Deliver whatever you say with confidence.
4. Get a favorable response to what you said.
5. Establish a precise follow-up action.
6. Make a great last impression.

With time, you really can carry out all of these steps during your call. I promise. I know because I do it myself.

But Here's the Catch

By my estimate you've got just eight short seconds to pull all of this off. I use this eight-second standard not because there's unanimity among my fellow sales experts and bestselling authors about exactly what constitutes the length of time necessary to leave a good first impression (there isn't), but because my own experience has proven to me that this is the outer limit for sales professionals. Believe me, I've made every mistake possible when it comes to initial approaches to prospects. So I know. Eight seconds really is all the time you have to get it done.

Now, if you're saying to yourself, "Hold it. Eight seconds doesn't seem like a very long time," try this simple experiment the next time you're out driving. After you hit a red light, just watch when the light turns green. Don't hit the accelerator. Keep your foot on the brake, and start counting: "One thousand one, one thousand two, one thousand three. . ."

By the time you get to "one thousand six," the person behind you will, in all likelihood, start to get out of his or her car to have a discussion with you. When you finally hit "one thousand eight," the intersection will be a symphony of honking horns, shouting mouths, and (shall we say) a pointing finger.

I believe you'll be convinced at this point that eight seconds can be a dreadfully long period of time, certainly long enough to do something intelligent with a conversation.

Now let's take a look at how you're going to take your six steps during that time.

Make a Great First Impression

If you're going to master this first step, you're going to have to become experienced at developing business rapport and being "likeable," someone others genuinely enjoy interacting with. This isn't as difficult as it may seem.

As a matter of fact, it can be fun. (Yep, you read it right—fun.) But that doesn't mean it's easy. Building business rapport is an acquired skill, one you must develop over time.

If I had to boil the art of business rapport-building into a single phrase, that phrase would probably be "equal business stature." Establishing equal business stature means approaching situations with your prospect as a partner (in the conversation, pending sale, everything), not as a supplicant or superior, no matter what her or his rank.

Salespeople who establish equal business stature with their suspects, prospects, customers, and business partners learn to understand the problems these people face and learn to present their own ideas in a way that the other person can understand. They're masters when it comes to building business rapport.

This is because establishing equal business stature is essentially the same thing as banishing fear from your relationship with your prospect.

Establishing equal business stature means understanding and responding empathetically and tactfully to the preconceptions people have about salespeople. Let's face it—prospects (and particularly very highly ranking prospects whom we've identified as Approvers, Decision Makers, and Influencers) are scared of you. They're afraid you're going to either

- waste their precious time, or
- talk about something with which they're not familiar.

The best way to overcome these fears from the other side is to calm down and develop a superlative opening statement. (That's what we'll have by the end of this chapter.) This opening statement will prove your value and make a point that's of importance to this buyer. You'll do this in three ways.

1. *By giving the person you're speaking with an idea that they will only get from you.* Imagine an Approver, Decision Maker, Influencer, and/or Recommender sitting in his or her office, cubicle, or whatever. The phone rings, and the person answers the phone. (I know, I know. That's not a given. I'll talk about voice mail later on.) Your contact hears the voice of someone he or she has not yet met, confidently offering an idea that they've not thought of themselves. If you play your cards right, the other person will think: Wow! I want to know more.

That's instant equal business stature. You're somebody in the know with new, fresh ideas.

How do you *get* these ideas? You get them from your customers and/or your own organization's Approver, Decision Makers, Influencers, and/or Recommenders, that's how. You get them from reading trade magazines, joining and participating in associations that pertain to your industry. You get them from showing up in your industry/niche or subgroup. (Remember when I was hyperventilating about all this stuff in Chapter Two? This is why.)

2. Ask the person you're speaking with a question that no one else will ask them. Imagine an Approver, Decision Maker, Influencer, and/or Recommender sitting by the phone. It rings. The person answers and hears you ask a question that gets them to think, a question that challenges him or her in a good way, a question that makes him or her think or say, "Now that's a good question."

That's equal business stature.

I am going to suggest that you incorporate the following questions into your first conversations:

- What's important to you personally about _____?
- Tell me more about _____.
- If you could change one aspect of _____, what would it be?
- What proof do you need to (see or hear) that would interest you enough to take a closer look at _____?
- What are your top three goals for _____ between now and _____ (some period of time)?
- What's the biggest problem you're having in _____?
- What improvements would you like to see in _____?
- Could you give me your opinion on _____?

> **Important Note:** In every case, you must fill in the blank with what's important to your prospect in his or her likely role as Approver, Decision Maker, Influencer, or Recommender. If you're not certain of what that something is, go back and reread the first five chapters of this wonderful, intellectual work.

3. By articulating whatever you say using words and phrases your prospects can easily identify with and understand. This is oh so very important. Perhaps the fastest way to totally turn off the interest of your prospect is to use words and phrases that are unfamiliar to the person you're speaking with.

No one likes to feel uninformed. If salespeople use unfamiliar words and phrases, they immediately challenge the other person's ego, power, control, and authority.

Don't do it. This is a universal law that applies to all humans in your sales territory.

Icebreakers

- "How are you today?"
- "Is this a good time?"
- "Do you have a few minutes?"
- "Hey, I just read about your company in the newspaper."
- "Your annual report says. . ."
- "Blah. Blah. Blah."

Here's some advice. Don't use icebreaker phrases in your cold calls. Don't use them in face-to-face visits, either. Icebreakers are for ships, not salespeople. They waste precious time, and they don't build business rapport, even if you think they do.

In the old days, icebreakers were supposedly used to reduce tension in a typical cold-call situation. Here's my question: Who's tense, anyway? Your prospect? I doubt it. Icebreakers are awkward, self-serving, inappropriate, and insulting.

Don't use them, either on the phone or in person.

A True Story

The following story is about icebreaker statements in a face-to-face meeting setting. The same principle applies to icebreakers you may be tempted to use during phone conversations.

As the young salesperson walks into the prospect's office, he takes a quick glance at a picture on the prospect's credenza. In a quick and somewhat careless move to make a great first impression and reduce tension, the rep says, "Wow. How did you manage to get your picture taken with John Madden?"

The prospect's answer ends the appointment and kills the sale:

"That's not John Madden. That's my wife."

Another True Story

I pick up the phone to call the CEO of one of the largest computer companies in the world. Much to my surprise, the CEO answers and says three stunning words, "This is Sam."

I respond with a lame attempt to build rapport:

"What a surprise! I expected your assistant."

Sam gives a classic CEO response, instant and right to the point:

"Hold on, I'll get her for you."

Click. Sound of phone ringing. Sound of assistant's voice-mail message.

That's one golden opportunity, gone forever.

Make Whatever You Say Sound Conversational

The fastest, easiest, and most reliable way for me to teach you how to do this is to suggest that you be authentic and speak with your prospect's purpose in mind. *Don't* use a script. No matter how hard you try, no matter how much practice and rehearsing you do to make a script sound unscripted, guess what? It will sound like you're reading.

By the end of this chapter, together we'll create an elevator pitch that you'll write, tape record, and then internalize. Once you internalize it—not word for word, but concept for concept, idea for idea—you'll throw away the script or tape recording, and never look at or listen to it again. When you call your prospects, you'll never, ever say it the same way twice. You'll be authentic in your approach, which means:

You won't be perfect; you won't even strive for perfection. That means you'll make mistakes. That means you won't take yourself too seriously. That means you'll be able to relax, smile, and yes, even chuckle a bit.

Deliver Whatever You Say with Confidence

Confidence—or faith, if you prefer—is the opposite of fear. With confidence is how super salespeople consistently respond to the inevitable challenges that come their way. Confidence is a way of thinking. Confidence is probably the single best way to reinsert fun into the sales process—even (especially) when you're up against a real challenge, like implementing your new No Cold-Calling sales model.

One great, fun way to build unshakable confidence is to hook up with other confident people on your sales team or in your community. For you, this may mean joining the local chapter of Toastmasters (a marvelous organization), enrolling in a local community college course on a topic of interest to you, listening to an audiotape series, or even attending a seminar conducted by a confident motivational speaker—like, say, me.

When all is said and done, your brain and its power can just as easily work against you as in your favor when it comes to developing personal confidence. This is because your brain does not know the difference between a negative and a positive phrase. It just takes the command and processes it, however it's delivered.

So for example, if you think, "I don't want to blow this call," your brain (and mine, too) hears: "Blow this call."

But if you think, "I'll make this call a massive success." Your brain (and, thankfully, mine, too) hears, "Massive success."

Here's a great confidence-building ritual related to your work on the phone. After every call you make, write down at least one part of the exchange that went well, as well as one part that you'd like to improve the next time around. Don't beat yourself up about what seemingly went wrong: visualize positive change. Command your mind with positive statements, and you'll usually find you have the energy to make them a reality.

The act of visualizing and thinking positive change constantly throughout the day is a consistent habit of superior salespeople who have confidence. Give it a try. You'll soon see that the seemingly "impossible" goals you set for yourself suddenly don't look quite so impossible.

Get a Favorable Response to What You Said

Let's set the stage. You're picking up the telephone to make the call. For right now, assume that you actually do get through to the person you're trying to reach. What could happen? A typical scenario might be the following.

Usually, when your prospect picks up the phone, that person will say his or her name: "This is Sally," or "Sam Bigdeal speaking." *Your first step will be to repeat this person's name.* Keep things formal. Use Mr. or Ms., and then the contact's last name. No, this is not a contradiction to building equal business stature and making a great first impression. Here's what it sounds like in action:

Prospect: "This is Sally."

You: "Ms. Jones?"

Prospect: "Yes."

Alternatively, you may hear:

Prospect: "Hello?" (Or "Facilities Management," "Extension 514," "Can I help you?")

You: "Ms. Jones?"

Prospect: "Yes."

At this point, you have Sally's undivided attention. Whatever she was doing prior to your saying her name, she's now stopped doing. She's paying attention to hear what you will say next.

Be very careful. What you say next will make all the difference.

What most salespeople do now—despite ample and endlessly repeated evidence that they shouldn't—is say something like this: "Hi, Ms. Jones. This is Will Perish with the ABC Insurance Company. Do you have a minute?"

Now, unless your name is Garth Brooks or Britney Spears, or your company affiliation is the IRS, I can tell you what's going to happen next.

The contact will respond to your self-defeating verbal blunder by tuning out.

Tuning out means asking you to send written information, repeating the sentence "I'm not interested" slowly and purposefully, pretending that the building just caught fire, or otherwise disengaging from the call. And giving you the gift of a dial tone.

So what have you got? You've only been on the line about a second and a half, and you're toast, a smoking English muffin. Game over.

So what do you do instead? What I am going to tell you now is going to be in direct conflict with what you've been taught to do during your sales training. I don't care. Do it anyway.

When Sally Jones says "Yes," or "Yes, this is Sally," you're going to respond with something confident, positive, and enthusiastic, something that does not directly identify you, your company, or the product or service you eventually want to discuss. It's too early in the relationship for you to pass along that kind of information. Instead, you're going to use a simple pleasantry. Take a look.

Prospect: "This is Sally."

You: "Ms. Jones?"

Prospect: "Yes."

You: "*It's great to finally speak with you.*"

Other possible pleasantries include:

- "Thanks for picking up the phone."
- "Thanks for taking my call."
- "It's an honor to speak with you."
- "It's such a surprise to get you on the phone."
- "It was a pleasure to read about (pertinent, positive news event relating to target company and/or Ms. Sally Jones)."

You get the idea. This will do a far better job for you than the act of volunteering your name and company affiliation at the outset of the conversation. Why? Because it's just too early. That's why.

What happens on the rare occasions when your contact says something like, "Hey, wait a minute. Who is this?" That's easy. Just say, "Oh, sorry, forgot to tell you. This is Will, Will Prosper, with the XYZ Insurance Company."

Or say, "Sorry, there's been so much excitement here at XYZ Insurance Company about our newest idea to increase employee retention and lower benefit costs that I forgot to tell you. It's Will, Will Prosper."

Then move on quickly and sure-footedly to the next phase.

The Hook, Grabber, USP, Bullet, and/or Sizzle

Immediately after your pleasantry, you're going to catch your prospect's attention by using a "hook" that's linked directly to something likely to be of interest to your contact whom, as you recall, will fall into one of four very different groups.

1. Leaders who want to hear about benefits.
2. Directors who want to hear about advantages.
3. Influencers who want to hear about features.
4. Recommenders who want to hear about functions.

The following is what a hook, grabber, USP, bullet, and/or sizzle for an Approver in the widget manufacturing industry might sound like.

Approver

Example 1

> *You:* "One of our ideas has increased revenues by as much as 4 percent while cutting expenses up to 12 percent in three months for six of the top-ten manufacturing organizations here in San Diego."

Example 2

> *You:* "One of our ideas has substantially increased revenues while dramatically cutting expenses in just three months for six of the top-ten manufacturing organizations here in San Diego."

Example 3

> *You:* "One of our ideas has increased employee satisfaction and reduced health-insurance claims in just three months for six of the top-ten manufacturing organizations here in San Diego."

(By the way: this is the heart of your elevator pitch, so called because it's brief enough to share between the second and third floors.)

You're most likely saying to yourself, "What does a grabber sound like for the other players I may choose to approach?"

Here ya go.

Decision Maker

> *You:* "Finding and resolving unintentional inefficiencies in [sales operations] is an area that we've become experts in. One example is

increasing return on sales while maintaining current budget levels for the coming year."

Critically Important Note 1: Make sure that somewhere in your grabber you mention this Decision Maker's line of business responsibility—in my example, sales operations.

Critically Important Note 2: Don't in any way, shape, or form ask obvious, stupid questions that will insult this Decision Maker, such as, "Tell me a little bit about your operations."

Influencer

You: "Our Matrix Three polarized optical scanner has a 99.9 percent retention factor and can provide optional features without costly contractor services."

Critically Important Note 1: Go easy on the success stories and/or name-dropping with your Influencer. Generally speaking, they're not keen on who's who unless the spotlight is on themselves.

Critically Important Note 2: If at all possible, give them choices, such as:

You: "We can investigate the probability of providing three different levels of interchangeability at the component, subassemble, and unit level. Which one is most important to you between now and the end of your current project?"

> **Critically Important Note 3:** Don't try to sell anything to the Influencer. They really don't like to be sold, and, truth be told, they can't buy anything. Buying is the Decision Maker and Approver's job.

Recommeder

You can include the following words in your grabber and win big with any Recommender:

- "Would it be helpful. . . ?"
- "Would it be useful. . . ?"
- "What would happen if. . . ?"
- "May I ask your opinion?"

You: "Would it be helpful if you could easily and quickly print your documents and send them without having to leave your work space?"

> **Critically Important Note 1:** Don't ask in any way, shape, or form for a decision. They can't make them.
>
> **Critically Important Note 2:** Your goal should be to find out as much as you can about what's going on in their world.

Five Things Your Hook Should Do

Your elevator pitch's hook—the heart of what you say—should accomplish five things. It should:

1. be rich in results.
2. be stated with what I call a "balanced gain-equation." (More on this in a minute.)
3. reference time.
4. introduce "social proof."
5. establish your all-important credibility and equal business stature.

Let's look at each of these in depth.

Rich in Results

There are two categories of results that just about every product, service, and solution ever created can deliver: tangible and intangible. We've talked about this already, so I won't go over it in detail again. Just remember: 1) that tangible results are easy to see and/or measure and should be expressed using numbers and/or percentages and 2) that intangible results cannot be measured definitively, may involve emotions or perceptions, and should be expressed using descriptive words and/or phrases.

Stated with a Balanced Gain-Equation

You'll never go wrong using a balanced gain-equation in describing what you sell. Here's why: Everyone here on planet Earth is motivated by one of two desires:

1. the desire to achieve a rewarding experience
2. the desire to avoid a painful experience

That's it. Simple, isn't it?

But what the heck is a balanced gain-equation?

Here's the point. By showing the upside and the downside of your idea (or whatever), you can appeal to both experiences. By doing so, it's a safe bet that you'll make your point relevant to the entire population.

Take another look at one of the statements I gave you, and you'll see that it balances both the securing of pleasure and the avoidance of pain.

> *You*: "One of our ideas has *increased revenues* by as much as 4 percent while *cutting expenses* up to 12 percent in three months for six of the top-ten manufacturing organizations here in San Diego."

In other words, you focus not just on how you increased revenues— but on how you did so "while cutting expenses." Do the research. Talk to your internal people. And figure out how to cover all your bases. Put together a series of case studies that balance the gain equation for your prospects.

Reference Time

Just about everything in business revolves around time, and just about everyone in business is concerned about time.

Therefore, when you make a statement of your ideas, capabilities, products, services, and/or solutions, you must include the element of time.

Specify the period of time it will likely take for *this* prospect to realize similar, or even greater, results.

Introduce Social Proof

Very few individuals fall into the category of what I call "early adopters." They are out there, but they're in the minority. Almost everyone wants to know that someone else has played pioneer, taken all the arrows, paved the way, posted results, and lived to talk about them. Social proof establishes the fact that you have "been there, done that, and gotten the T-shirt." There are three ways for you to introduce social proof:

1. Verbalize a direct quote from a happy existing customer: "Ima Bigshot, at Stellar Products, increased her new-product revenue by as much as 12 percent while cutting up to 53 percent off time to market in just nine months."

2. Use a direct quote from the leader or line-of-business executive in *your* organization: "Our CEO is personally inviting you to find out how we may be able to help increase your new-product revenue by as much as 12 percent, while compressing your time to market by up to 53 percent in as little as nine months. That's why you're hearing from me today."

3. Use a relative-ranking name-drop: "One of our ideas has increased revenues by as much as 4 perecent while cutting expenses up to 12 percent in three months for six of the top-ten manufacturing organizations here in San Diego."

The third social-proof option, relative ranking, is the safest. You'll never be able to predict how your prospect reacts to your other customers. Who knows? She or he may have just lost a big deal to Stellar Products, your bread-and-butter account.

Establish All Important Credibility and Equal Business Stature

Believe it. If you do everything I've laid out, as I've laid it out, you will win credibility and equal business stature.

Now, before we proceed to the next part of our elevator pitch, let me warn you about something. At the moment you articulate your hook, something extraordinary may happen. You may get interrupted by whomever you happen to be speaking to.

This is a good thing.

The Interruption

If your hook is doing its job, your prospect is likely to cut in and say something like:

- "This sounds familiar. Did you send me a letter about this?"
- "This sounds interesting. Tell me all about it."
- "I think I read something about your company."
- "I haven't heard of this before, but I must admit it sounds vaguely interesting."
- "I have absolutely no interest."

Don't worry. You'll be learning how to deal with all of these interruptions, including that scary-sounding, trip wire last one, later on in the book. For now, just remember that your objective is to keep the prospect engaged. If that's not happening after one or two attempts at initiating person-to-person discourse, say "Thank you" and move on.

You may also decide to use the final element of your elevator pitch, which I'll get to in just a minute.

Naming Names

Once you've shared your hook, your prospect knows the reason for your call. The cat's out of the bag. *This* is the perfect time to identify yourself—not beforehand. If you'd like, you can also identify your organization. If you choose to identify your employer, say a little bit about what makes it great. Remember, though, that whatever you say has to fit into one brief sentence. It should sound pretty darn close to this:

> *You:* "This is Will, Will Prosper, with ABC Insurance Company, the hardest-working company in the insurance industry today."

The Ending Question of Your Elevator Pitch

If you don't get interrupted, you're going to conclude your elevator pitch with an ending question that incorporates some element of time. It should run no longer than two sentences. In each of the ending questions below, you'll probably want to say your prospect's name at the beginning. Here's what it might sound like:

> *You:* "Ms. Bigshot, does this touch on issues that are of concern to you this (month/year/quarter)?"

Alternatively:
- "Is this something you'd like to explore further?"
- "What are your thoughts right now?"
- "Have I touched on an issue that affects your day-to-day operations?"
- "Who besides you would you like me to speak with about our ideas before the end of this week?"

Let's Put It All Together

Here's an example of an elevator pitch that works. Of course, yours shouldn't sound *exactly* like this one. Remember, you'll be creating yours and internalizing it, but it should be about this long. And it should, like what follows, hit all the bases you've been reading about.

> This particular elevator pitch is directed toward an Approver in your prospect's organization. Remember, your aim is to use your pitch to win interest and attention, typically by eliciting some significant comment or interruption. You're not trying to compete with the prospect for the right to talk. You're not trying to finish your statement. And remember, you'll be following the written wave you created in Chapter Eleven.

Your prospect picks up his phone and says: "Good morning, this is Jay. How can I help you?"

You: "Mr. Strikeitrich, it was a pleasure to read that your company has successfully expanded into the European marketplace. By the way, after studying another client's operation, we suggested an idea that provided revenue gains of over $25,000 per year. The real surprise is that we did this without taking one bit of its hard-earned capital. This is Will, Will Prosper, at Zenith. Mr. Strikeitrich, their impressive results may be tough to duplicate. But would you be willing to take the next step between now and the first of the year to find out if we could help you create similar or even greater results?"

139

Again, you shouldn't try to insert your company's annual report (or Mr. Strikeitrich's) into these opening remarks. You should use all the ideas I've given you so far in this chapter, combine them with your function (for the Recommender), feature (for the Influencer), advantage (for the Decision Maker), and benefit (for the Approver), and make the pitch your own.

Establish a Precise Follow-Up Action
When it comes to following up on your first interaction with your prospect (or any other interaction you may have with them), the two most critical words are "do it." And I strongly suggest that you do it *sooner* than you promised, rather than later. Doesn't matter what it happens to be: sending additional information, providing a referral name and telephone number, sending an e-mail, or hammering out a thanks-for-your-time handwritten note. Whenever you mail, e-mail, drop off, or have someone else deliver anything, make sure you call whomever you sent it to and confirm that they have received it. Enough said.

Make a Great Last Impression
Contrary to popular belief, you have two chances to make an impression—at the beginning of your interaction with your prospect and at the end, be it over the telephone or during an in-person meeting.

On the Telephone
Your elevator pitch should allow you to create a great first impression. Let's say that you're speaking with an Influencer, and she's the head civil engineer for a large construction firm that has just been awarded a contract to build a water recovery system. You can make a great last impression at the end of your telephone conversation by saying something like:

> *You:* "Thanks for your time today. I'll e-mail you the research paper that highlights our specific capabilities, and the next time we speak, I would really enjoy hearing about your firsthand experience during your Salt River Project. I've heard that your organization got the Contractor-of-the-Year award."

It's been my experience that the prospect will say something like, "Why wait until then? I've got a minute right now."

In Person

As I mentioned earlier, the elevator pitch can be used in person as well for ensuring that you make your best first impression. Let's say that your first in-person appointment in this organization happens to be with the Decision Maker. As you're leaving her office, you can say:

> *You:* "Thank you for your time today. I'll make sure that I drop off the competitive outsourcing information that you're interested in, and by the way, at that time I would love for you to explain how you were able to become the youngest female executive vice president in your company's history."

Here again, it's been my experience that you'll hear something pretty darn close to: "Here, have a seat, and let me tell you. . . ."

In Conclusion

Start your first interaction with each and every prospect you meet with a high-impact elevator pitch as I've outlined in this chapter. And conclude your first interaction on a high note by asking something of an important personal/professional nature in a very sincere way. You'll quickly be joining the ranks of the top producing salespeople in your organization, if not the nation.

Now You Do It!

Take a moment, and a deep breath. Put this book to one side. Grab a piece of paper and a pencil, and develop your own elevator pitch right now.

> Don't continue with this book until you've done this. I am not kidding. This is critically important to your total success with your No Cold-Calling model.

Have you got a first draft? Good. You're now ready to move on to the next chapter.

Six Big Ideas

When following up on your correspondence wave with a telephone call, build and practice an elevator pitch that:

1. Makes a great first impression.

2. Makes whatever you say sound conversational.

3. Delivers whatever you say with confidence.

4. Gets a favorable response to what you said.

5. Establishes precise follow-up action.

6. Makes a great last impression.

Don't forget to go to www.stopcoldcalling.info for additional for-fee information. Click on "Chapter Twelve: Online Assets."

Notes

Notes

NO COLD-CALLING
PRINCIPLE 13

"You'll always be sent to
the person you sound
the most like."

—E8486

CHAPTER THIRTEEN

Roadblocks

BEFORE GETTING STARTED WITH THIS ALL-IMPORTANT CHAPTER, I WANT TO underscore the importance of two individuals that you'll be in contact with before you ever get to speak with your target prospect. They are the receptionist gatekeeper and the administrative-assistant gatekeeper. Their job is to make sure that you (and I) and every other salesperson calling the company gets connected with the right resource. Contrary to popular sales belief, they are not waiting for us to "make their day" by rejecting us. When you treat these all-important players with respect and state your well-founded purpose, your call will be put through to the person you sound the most like. And if you've been following my advice, you'll sound like the consummate business professional you were meant to be.

Of course, not everyone you talk to will give you an appointment; that's simply the nature of sales. But if you use the system I'm laying out for you, most everyone you talk to will give you a good idea about whether or not he or she is interested in making the transition from prospect to customer.

Gatekeepers

If you're planning to make telephone calls or in-person visits, you'll be running into two very different types of gatekeepers. It's vitally important that you learn to distinguish between the two. They are:

1. Receptionist gatekeepers, and
2. Administrative-assistant gatekeepers.

Receptionist Gatekeepers

These people are the front line of the organization's "defense." However, their goal is not, as you might sometimes think, to make the salesperson's life a living hell. It's to make sure calls are routed quickly and efficiently to the proper individual. If this results in you (or me) feeling like _____ [use your own word here], that's our problem, not theirs.

For the most part, receptionist gatekeepers are pleasant, helpful individuals who are truly interested in making sure the right people get connected with one another. Over the years, salespeople have given these folks more than their fair share of grief by:

- Asking endless questions.
- Trying to engage in long-winded discussions.
- Stretching the truth (or worse).
- Claiming to know people they don't.
- Adopting a smug or condescending manner.
- Not answering the gatekeepers.

Don't do any of that stuff. These mistakes will undermine your career growth in both the short and long term, and they won't get you any closer to the people you want to talk to.

Instead, follow these two simple rules in your dealings with receptionist gatekeepers:

1. Always tell the truth.
2. Don't get huffy if the person asks, "What's the call about?"

In fact, the fastest way to get connected to the person you're trying to reach is to tell the gatekeeper receptionist exactly what the call *is* about. I am fully aware that this contradicts just about everything you and I have ever learned about getting over, around, past, under, and through these individuals. Ignore all of that stuff. All you have to do is deliver a (slightly compressed) version of a portion of your elevator pitch—the one you've prepared for the person you're trying to reach. What you say may or may not make any sense to the gatekeeper receptionist. This gives us two possible scenarios.

1. The busy receptionist understands exactly what you're talking about. In the majority of cases, your call will go right through to your target person.
2. The busy receptionist will have little to no idea what you're talking about, but will understand *who* you want to talk to. In the majority of cases, your call will go right through to your target person.

Sounds like a win-win plan, don't you think?

It sounds like this:

Receptionist Gatekeeper: "Good Morning, ABC Company. How may I direct your call?"

You: "This is Will Prosper. Would you please connect me with Mr. Gladstone? Thank you."

Receptionist Gatekeeper: "What's the call about?"

You: "An idea that Mr. Gladstone can use that can possibly provide revenue gains of over $25,000 per year—without taking one bit of hard-earned capital—that we've accomplished for another organization that Mr. Gladstone may know about. Would you please connect me? Thank you."

The Golden Rule Rules

Your call will go through if, and only if, you sound like the person you're asking to be connected to. In other words, if you want to talk to an Approver, you need to sound like an Approver. Consider this extremely unfortunate scenario:

Receptionist Gatekeeper: "Good Morning, ABC Company. How may I direct your call?"

You: "This is Will Perish. Would you please connect me with Mr. Gladstone? Thank you."

Receptionist Gatekeeper: "What's the call about?"

You: "I represent the largest manufacturer of high-performance widget testing devices, and I'd like to talk with Mr. Gladstone about our organization. Would you please connect me? Thank you."

Receptionist Gatekeeper: "Right. Well, Mr. Gladstone doesn't handle that sort of thing and anyway, he doesn't take calls from salespeople. Our purchasing department conducts all business with vendors. Hold on. I'll connect you with Wilber Paineintheneck, our purchasing manager."

or

Receptionist Gatekeeper: "Our purchasing department takes care of all sales calls. Hold on. I'll connect you with Wilber Paineintheneck, our purchasing manager."

Yes, I know. It hurt to read that. Moral of the story:

Sound like Mr. Gladstone, and you stand a much better chance of talking to Mr. Gladstone.

Administrative-Assistant Gatekeepers

If you're trying to reach Approvers and/or Decision Makers, you'll most likely spend some time talking to the trusted administrative-assistant gatekeeper.

The vast majority of salespeople make a fatal mistake here. They turn these people into enemies. Don't do that. The administrative assistant, as a general rule, knows all, sees all, and controls all access. (Truth be told, many of them are better informed and more on top of things than their bosses are.) The administrative assistant is not a person you want to tick off.

There is one simple rule to keep in mind when dealing with the administrative assistant who works for an Approver or Decision Maker. It is:

Treat this person exactly the way you'd treat the Approver and/or Decision Maker.

No exceptions, no variations, no kidding. It's a bit of a mistake to say this person is the power behind the throne. The administrative assistant is, not infrequently, the power *on* the throne, in that he or she takes over and runs the line of business or company when the leader isn't there. (Truth be told, quite a few of them run the show when the leader *is* there.) So treat these people with the respect they deserve.

Believe it. Whenever an administrative assistant answers the phone, you have, for all intents and purposes, reached your high-level prospect. Launch into your elevator pitch. The only change you'll make will be to use the administrative assistant's name instead of the Approver's and/or Decision Maker's. (You'll want to confirm both names—that of your target person and his or her administrative assistant—before you make this call. You can do that by checking the Web site or by calling the front desk.)

The downside to this approach? There is one. The administrative assistant can reject you. But guess what? He or she can do that anyway. So you might as well be nice, show the respect that they are due, and be the success you were meant to be.

The upside to this approach? By making your statement directly to this all-important gatekeeper, you'll:

- win respect and business rapport with the administrative assistant.
- convince the administrative assistant that your ideas are sound.
- in the vast majority of cases, *earn the right to speak to the boss.*
- become the success that you were meant to be.

Try It. You've Got Everything to Gain and Nothing to Lose

Most salespeople make no distinction between the two types of gate-keepers, and simply try to bully or smooze their way through. My approach to dealing with these two (very different) members of your prospect's organization takes all the conflict and misery out of interactions with gatekeepers. It lets you get where you need to be, which is on the receptionist gatekeeper's and administrative-assistant gatekeeper's good side.

That's a desirable destination, because these people control your access to key players—and thus your income.

Voice Mail Jail

Voice mail is just a tool for you and me to use to take the sales process to the next highest level. In other words, if you can't leave a compelling reason for your prospect to return your call, you shouldn't leave any message. Period.

Treat voice mail like a person-to-person interaction.

Like it or not, you'll apt to voice mail about 50 percent of the time. So don't be surprised or disappointed when this happens. You really don't need to remember any kind of script or special approach. Just use my signature "bookend" approach, which employs an authentic, casual intro and outro. Take a look:

> *"Mr. Greatguy, if you were in your office to take my call this is what you would've heard. This is Will Prosper, with CoolCo. Would you be willing to give me your opinion on an idea that [65 of the* Fortune *100] find valuable, and that's proven to [increase the size of every initial sale by as much as 54 percent—while at the same time cutting sales-process time by up to one-half?] If so, you can reach out to me any afternoon between [3:00 and 5:00 P.M.] I look forward to hearing your response and understanding your level of interest. My number is [800-777-8486. That's 800-777-8486.] Thanks for listening, and have a great rest of the day."*

Your Voice Is More Powerful Than Your Message

You cannot control what your prospect's reaction to your elevator pitch or voice-mail message may be, but there are four important elements that are under your direct control whenever you pick up the telephone to talk to a prospect. The envelope, please. You can control

- your tone.
- your modulation.
- your volume.
- your pacing.

Tone

The tone you use will determine how easy (or difficult) it will be for the person on the other end of the line to process your message.

Contrary to popular belief, your tone can be changed. The natural and most appealing tone of your voice is actually the tone of your hum. This probably isn't the vocal tone you (or I) habitually use during conversations. The secret to finding and using your natural voice is simply to practice a little each day by picking your favorite song and humming a bar, then singing that same bar. Pick the same song for several days in a row, and then change the song. Do this until your natural voice appears in all of your conversations without thinking about it, whether on the telephone or in other situations.

Modulation

What works best is to modulate your voice to the topic and emotions of your discussion. When something is important or you're asking a question, your modulation should vary.

If you're looking for guidance on this score, close your eyes and listen to one of the nightly network news anchors deliver their latest story of demise and disaster. Generally speaking, you'll want to *raise* the pitch of your voice during the last few words when asking a question and *lower* the pitch of your voice during the last few words when making a statement of fact.

Volume

We learned to follow a simple principle while we were children: the more important your point is, the louder your voice should be. This is a big mistake.

In a professional setting, your volume should remain totally constant. Period. Judicious use of silence—or modulation of tone or pitch—are the best ways to emphasize a point.

Pacing

The speed at which you speak *must* match the speaking speed of your prospect. Here are some general guidelines:
- *Approvers.* Assume fastest-paced delivery.
- *Decision Makers.* Assume second-fastest-paced delivery.
- *Influencers.* Assume slower-paced delivery.
- *Recommenders.* Assume slowest-paced delivery.

Avoid, at all costs, making your calls from cell phones. (They're dangerously close to being inaudible.) Also avoid using headsets, even an expensive one. (They're only marginally better.)

No Log

As you make calls to your prospects keep a No Log. Yep, each and every time you get a response, such as:

- "No."
- "I've got no interest."
- "Get lost."
- "Take a hike."

Write down the exact time of day it happened, the exact words, and any other form of *no* your prospects come up with. Then toward the end of your day, review your log. Call back the first no of your day and say:

"Mr. Cutmeoff, earlier today, at 9:30 in the morning, you said to me that you had no interest in my ideas. Let me ask you, have you had a change of heart since then?"

Sounds ridiculous, I know. But guess what? My experience is that I've gotten between 10 and 20 percent of my previous no's to say something pretty darn close to:

"You know, this morning I was in a rush. Tell me what's on your mind."

Bingo! No Cold Calling pay dirt.

Eight Big Ideas

1. Your call will go through if, and only if, you sound like the person you're asking to be connected to.

2. When dealing with administrative gatekeepers, treat the person exactly the way you'd treat the Approver and/or Decision Maker.

3. Treat voice mail like a person-to-person interaction.

4. Control your tone.

5. Control your modulation.

6. Control your volume.

7. Control your pacing.

8. Call back people who say "no" that very day, and ask them if they've had a change of heart.

Don't just sit there. Let's get on to the next chapter.

Notes

NO COLD-CALLING PRINCIPLE 14

"The shortest way to a sale

is with a referral."

—E8486

CHAPTER FOURTEEN

Referrals

S O WHAT'S THE PAYOFF FROM THE STUFF YOU'VE LEARNED SO FAR?
It's a fair question. Let's take a look at the numbers.

My research shows that contacting prospects (individuals and organizations that fit your TIP), using the tools you've learned about so far in this book, will yield on average a 25 percent contact-to-appointment ratio.

In other words, if you reach out to 100 prospects, you'll get as many as 25 appointments. That's pretty good shooting. One thing's for sure: That number is *dramatically* better than the number you'll get by "dialing for dollars" the old-fashioned way. ("Hi, my name is. . ." "How are you today?" "Have I caught you at a bad time?")

On the other hand, when you incorporate the tactics in this book to call high-quality referral prospects, your efforts will yield, on average, a staggering 40 percent ratio.

You read right. Make 100 connections to referrals, and you'll get somewhere in the neighborhood of 40 appointments. What's more, industry research shows that individuals who buy from you and who fall into the "referred prospect" category are 2.5 times more likely to give you a referral, a referral that will, of course, yield a 40 percent chance of return.

Finally, a sales monster that feeds itself—and is totally on your side.

> Lots of salespeople (and too many sales managers) seem to think that selling starts with your first contact with the prospective buyer—and ends when you receive a signature on a purchase order. There's a lot of selling work that can and should happen before that first contact—and also after the ink dries on the P. O. (purchase order, of course). Now it's time you learn about some of the most important sales work in the world—how to build unshakable loyalty by asking for, and getting, referrals worth their weight in gold.

Why We Go to Work Every Day

Customers are the reason we show up for work every morning, the reason our company exists. As important as it is to persuade prospects to turn into new customers, it's also important to be sure that the solutions you've delivered are being used by, and are of benefit to, the people who are already your customers.

Picture your customer sitting on a three-legged stool and holding a fistful of referrals. If for any reason one leg gives way, the whole thing comes tumbling down. Your customer winds up on the floor—along with your referrals.

Customers who have the supports kicked out from under them don't usually come back. Instead, they vote with their feet and quietly go somewhere else, taking your pot of gold with them.

There are three vitally important legs supporting your relationship and winning those golden referrals that lead you to more customers.

1. Trust
2. Expectations
3. Investments

Trust

When you tell your customer something, is it the truth, the whole truth, and nothing but the truth? Do you keep your word no matter what—and let your customers know ahead of time on those rare occasions when a projection, delivery, installation, or whatever suddenly looks unrealistic? Do you always, without fail, determine what is in your customer's best interests and then act in accordance with those interests?

Trust is absolutely essential in any meaningful business relationship, whether you're selling computers, designer clothing, cosmetics, chemicals, or accounting services. What makes trust happen? The authority of your word, for one thing.

If you state something definitively and then make a habit of coming back and overruling yourself because of the people "back at headquarters," your trust is going to take a hit, no matter how earnest or innocent your initial statements were.

So think before you speak. Never give any prospect or customer reason to doubt the authority of your word. When a customer asks something about which you may not yet have all the facts, *say so*. Keep the customer's trust. Say something like: "This is such an important issue that I want to do a little research for you and get it right. I'll get the answer from the person in my organization who's directly responsible for this area, and I'll report back to you no later than Thursday by phone."

Then (you guessed it), keep your word.

Expectations

Many salespeople, I'd venture to guess a solid majority, work a lot harder at setting up customer expectations than they do at fulfilling them. Don't make that mistake.

If you promise a result to your customer, put it in writing and make it clear, after the sale, that you intend to do anything and everything necessary to turn it into a reality. I recommend monthly or quarterly progress reports, delivered in person *and* on paper.

Sometimes customers develop unrealistic expectations because salespeople make completely unintentional, and usually pretty vague, statements that customers choose to interpret in ways that are convenient to them. Although this type of miscommunication isn't exactly dishonest, it can result in outcomes that are just as catastrophic as when salespeople lie through their teeth.

Set realistic expectations. Make sure they're crystal clear. Put them in writing. Go over them in a face-to-face meeting with your customer.

Investments

Your customers will expect a return on every investment they make by working with you. If they don't get a return, then what they thought was an investment turns into a loss. And guess what? They won't return.

> **News Flash:** Relationships that your customers associate with financial losses don't fall into the mutually beneficial category and won't win you referrals.

You and your organization must prove—not just once, not just twice, not just this quarter, but continually—that a return on investment is taking place. And if a return on investment isn't taking place, then you have to take personal responsibility for changing what needs to be changed until one does take place.

Ten Commandments of Referral Generation

Getting a referral is a quantifiable, repeatable process. Once you get the basic principles down, you'll be able to repeat the process and achieve a predictable result—get the referral and aspire to the 40 percent level you deserve. Once you get the basic principles down, you'll *want* to ask for referrals. That's a promise. The following Ten Commandments have served me so well over the years that I am going to urge you to read them at least once each and every week.

1. Understand your customer on a business level first.

This is the beginning point. If you don't do this, you won't have a customer, period.

2. Understand your customer on a personal level.

What drives this person? Makes him or her happy? Gets him or her riled up? Makes him or her cackle with glee?

Each and every person on the face of this Earth is unique and distinct in the sight of the Creator, but for some reason we salespeople have a disturbing habit of treating Contact A, who faces business problems similar to those of Contact B, as though he or she were Contact B.

Find out what special, distinctive, personal approaches your contact takes to business and to life in general. How does this person make decisions? Express opinions? Measure success? Set goals? What hobbies, sports, and avocations make this person's life more interesting?

The more you know, the better positioned you'll be to develop a truly meaningful relationship with each and every one of your customers, and that will lead you to the pot of golden referrals that they have for you.

3. Understand the products, services, and solutions they sell.

Understanding what your customer's organization sells is just as important as understanding what you sell. Here are some ideas on how you can make this understanding a reality.

- Make every possible attempt to use whatever it is that your customer sells.
- Make every possible attempt to talk to a few of your customer's customers.
- Make every possible attempt to purchase one share of stock in each of your customer's organizations.
- Make yourself available to attend any and all of your customer's meetings that involve discussions of what you've sold.
- Make every attempt to invite key players within your own organization to visit with your customers so that they, too, can get an insight into your customer's world.
- Meet as many Decision Makers within their organization as you possibly can.

- Read and frequently review your customer's mission statement.

4. Understand how to add value beyond what you sold them.

This can be tricky, but it's essential. You'll have to do some digging and become what I call a *thought partner* to pull this one off. Here's how it works.

First, look beyond what you sold this customer and ask yourself: What other problems does this customer have that I may be of assistance in solving that do not involve my products, services, or solutions? Once you come up with an area or two, you'll have to find other salespeople and organizations that can solve those needs. To make this easier and less of a risk consider:

- Contacting your own organization's suppliers.
- Contacting suppliers of your other customers.
- Joining a professional networking organization. Typically, these people and the organizations they represent are reliable, creditable, and won't disappoint you or your customer.

5. Show up for every single customer meeting on time.

"Tony," you ask, "isn't this one pretty obvious? Isn't it second nature not to keep a customer waiting?" Yep. It's obvious. And maybe it should be second nature. But plenty of salespeople still let this one slide. Why? It's easy to get busy, darn busy, in this crazy business world of ours. All the same, there's very little that gets your customers more irritated than having to cool their heels while they wait for you.

So this point is worth emphasizing and re-emphasizing on a daily (or hourly) basis. Don't be late for anything that involves your customer. End of story.

6. Show up at every single customer meeting, prepared to address the topics on the agenda.

If your customer expects you to be in attendance at a meeting, it behooves you to find out what it's about ahead of time. Don't waste everyone's time, effort, and energy by staring around the table blank-eyed and repeating the mantra of the unprepared: "Let me look into that for you." The more you can look into *before* the meeting, the more answers you'll be able to provide. The more answers you provide, the happier your customer will

160

be. You know where this is going: The happier your customers are, the more referrals you'll get.

7. Drop in without an appointment rarely, and only when there is something of significant value to discuss.

Yes, there are some situations where dropping in without an appointment makes sense as part of your initial contact method. But we're not talking about getting a share of the contact's attention now; we're talking about managing a relationship over the long term. That means respecting your customer's time. Never drop by for a chat because you happen to be in a customer's area. Use the means of contact for which your customer expresses a personal preference. In other words, ask customers what touch point appeals to them. When in doubt, always set up an appointment ahead of time.

8. Be proactive.

This is a biggie. Being proactive in any relationship proves that you're a responsible partner. Here's how you can do it for your customers:

- Have a physical and electronic file for each of your customers. Use a table of contents for each customer file that shows what is of interest to them.
- As you read the local newspapers, trade rags, and/or the many e-zines that come your way, cut out anything you see that may be of interest to customers and paste it into their files.
- Send it to them or deliver your "I thought you'd be interested in this" information on a regular basis.
- Scan your own company's new product releases and future visions and keep your customers informed.
- Invite line-of-business executives from your organization to visit with your customers, either virtually or in person.
- Get your noncompeting customers together (here again, either virtually or in person) on a regular basis.

9. Follow up ahead of time.

We touched on this in a previous chapter. Live by the rule: "Underpromise and over-deliver." Don't wait until the last minute. Don't procrastinate.
    'Nuff said.

10. Return phone calls promptly.

"I can't possibly return all these calls by the end of the day."

You're right. You probably can't. Let's face it. A typical sales day includes more action items than you actually have time to complete. That means you'll need to prioritize your activities and not just "push the pile forward."

So let's get real. Some of the messages you receive from customers will fall into the "call me when you can" category; others will fall into the "emergency" category. Just make sure you're not putting off returning calls in the latter category.

I use the following categories to classify incoming messages:

- *Urgent.* Must be returned within two hours.
- *Critical.* Must be returned the same working day.
- *Important.* Must be returned by the next working day.
- *Casual.* Should be returned as soon as a slot arises.

Customers count on you to be there to talk to when things get weird, and if you don't come through for them, they won't come through for you. Remember, it's their checks that keep the lights on in your office and their referrals that will get you into the ranks of a 40 percent contact-to-appointment ratio. So adopt some way (you can take my example above if you like), and use it. Let your customers know how it works and ask them to put their request for your time and attention into the appropriate category.

By the way, if you're the kind of person who likes to leave personalized and date-stamped messages on your voice-mail system, make sure it's always up to date:

"You've reached Jill Somers' voice-mail box. For today, May 14, I'll be out of the office with clients all day. Please leave a message, and I'll return your call. Thanks, and have a great rest of the day."

Just make sure you keep it up-to-date.

Serve Up a Good Dose of ROI

ROI is what the customer gets in return for investing in your organization's products, services, and solutions—above and beyond the investment itself. If what you sold them causes more problems than it solves or delivers results that do not defray the costs associated with working with you, then it has not delivered any return on investment.

162

Generally speaking, there are three general categories of ROI:

1. *Hard-value/tangible ROI.* After a little research, this is easy to see and easy to measure. This is the direct, quantifiable impact your solution has had on the organization in your area of activity. Examples of hard-value ROI would include increases in revenue, earnings, income, margin, or market share that can be directly traced to (for instance) the sales training you offer, or decreases in taxes, expenses, staffing expenses, or overdue debt that can be directly traced to (for instance) the accounting services you offer. Hard-value ROI is generally measured, expressed, and articulated in numbers and percentages.

2. *Soft-value/intangible ROI.* This is harder to see and measure, but nevertheless represents significant advances in areas of direct relevance to your customer and his or her organization. Examples of soft-value ROI would include improvements in customer relations, market exposure, or image management, or a decrease in worries, problems, or risk in some other area of your customer's business or personal life. Soft-value ROI is usually measured and expressed by using descriptive words and phrases: "The possibility of negative media coverage on X issue has now been substantially eliminated, thanks to the strategies we've put into place."

3. *Emotional ROI.* This is easy to observe, but hard to measure. Emotional ROI is sometimes referred to as the "emotional paycheck" accompanying a particular course of action. Usually, emotional ROI takes the form of internal feelings of pride, acceptance, recognition, prestige, and social status; it could also include a greater feeling of love, or increased self-esteem. As you can see, emotional ROI deals with internal wealth and richness of life.

There are only four ways to measure the ROI of what you're selling. They are, in order of preference:

1. You work with your customers and get a commitment from them to collect the information, assess it, and generate a (formal or informal) report. Despite what you might be thinking now, many of your customers will be highly motivated to take this step because they, too, will want to know how well your product, service, or solution is

working. Don't panic. Fear not. Your organization would have an Out of Business sign in the window if it wasn't delivering results.

2. You take the initiative and (perhaps while at the customer's facility) personally collect all the information, assess it, and generate a report of your own that your customer either revises or signs off on. This approach will help you handle those customers who simply don't have the time or resources to track down the information you need to determine your ROI.

3. You make a responsible estimate of the ROI without collecting hard data, an estimate based on substantial industry experience or trend analysis, then get your customer to either revise it or sign off on it. This approach will allow you to handle customers who are uncomfortable with either of the above techniques.

4. This last measurement is relevant only if you are measuring emotional ROI. Get up close and personal with your customers, and discuss their emotional response to what you sell, as friends would. Level with one another. Don't expect this type of connection to emerge with everyone you sell to. It takes time and is actually pretty rare.

If It Ain't Working Better Than They Expect—Fix It

- Any attempt to follow these instructions. . .
- Any attempt to quantify the ROI you deliver to your customer. . .
- Any attempt to determine whether or not what you're offering represents an appreciating asset for your customer. . .

You may turn up some not so pleasant situations that suggest that what you sold this customer is not working at peak performance.

If this is the case, celebrate. You've just uncovered a great opportunity to fix things and improve the relationship. Doing so will build your credibility in the eyes of your customer. As a matter of fact, if you're looking for an easy way to *guarantee* your customer's cooperation in determining ROI, you can position your request as a performance evaluation of your equipment (or whatever else you've sold them), to make sure that what they've paid for is in fact up to par.

Getting the Referrals

Once you've taken to heart and put into action everything that we've talked about so far in this chapter—and not before—you will be ready to ask your customer for a referral. I am going to show you *who* to ask, *when* to ask, and *how* to ask so you, too, can enjoy the appointment ratios I talked about in the first few sentences of this chapter. Before we begin, here are some of the areas that have proven to be fruitful for me over the years in generating referrals:

- Suppliers   (and their suppliers and customers)
- Outsourcers (and their suppliers and customers)
- Customers   (and their suppliers and customers)
- Affiliates   (and their suppliers and customers)
- Distributors   (and their suppliers and customers)
- Sister organizations (and their suppliers and customers)
- Parent organizations (and their suppliers and customers)
- Board members (and their suppliers and customers)
- Other divisions (and their suppliers and customers)
- Your own company (and their suppliers and customers)

I hope you will review the list carefully and put it to good use. For instance, notice that outsourcing companies are everywhere these days. Let's say that you sell network routers and ancillary equipment. You're calling on a large manufacturing company, and you discover that its entire data center, including a server farm, is being maintained and operated by ADE, a major outsourcing organization. Guess what? You just hit No Cold-Calling pay dirt. Why? Because they're a major user and player in your niche. Get a referral that will point you toward ADE's Approver, Decision Maker, and Influencer, and you'll be well on your way to over-quota performance.

Or consider that many organizations have a board of directors. And just about every board member is an Approver in some other organization. If you are providing any worthwhile service (and I know that you are), don't you think that the board members of your existing customer's organization would like to know about it? As a matter of fact, if you do nothing other than establish business relationships with the board members of each of your existing customers, you might be able to generate enough referrals to last the rest of your sales career.

See the trend?

How about this? Each and every company in business has suppliers and customers, or they wouldn't be in business. Once you tap into *this* base of referrals you'll be done with cold calling *Forever*. Imagine the power of calling up the supplier of one of your best customers—a customer you have *demonstrated* your value to—and saying something like the following: "Mr. Peters, Jan Roberts at PCT Products, your biggest customer in the Portland area, suggested that I give you a call."

Mr. Peters just stopped whatever he was doing and now is glued to the next words that come out of your mouth. *Cha-ching.*

Whom to Ask

It's not likely that an Approver will give you a referral to a Recommender or Influencer. However, it's very likely that an Approver, when asked at the correct time in an appropriate way, will refer you to another Approver. In other words, like-to-like applies whenever you're asking for referrals.

Make a habit of asking for referrals at each and every level (Approver, Decision Maker, Influencer, and Recommender) of each and every organization you're currently doing business with.

Your Greatest Obstacle

The thought of actually asking for referrals generates plenty of excuses from salespeople. Here are some of the most common.

- "It's not the right time."
- "I don't think that she or he knows anyone who can use what I sell."
- "It's too sales-y."
- "My prospect doesn't share that kind of information with salespeople."
- "That kind of information is company confidential, and I can't ask my prospect to break the rules."
- "I don't need to ask. They'll offer if I wait long enough."

All this chatter is a smoke screen for something much more basic: Fear! This is the greatest obstacle to generating referrals. We're freaked out that our request will be denied and we'll get rejected. It's our biggest obstacle. Here's what I suggest doing to overcome it.

Know in your heart of hearts that asking for a referral will:

- make the person you are asking a hero in the eyes of the person you're referred to.
- create a deeper relationship and greater loyalty between you and the person you're asking for a referral.

Your existing customers' and prospects' loyalty to you really will increase tenfold with every referral you ask them for. Why? Because with each and every referral they give you, they get a little more committed to you. It's not likely that your prospect/customer will introduce you to someone they know and then cut you loose.

Keep Asking for Referrals

The frequency with which you ask your prospects and customers for referrals should be tied to your regular account reviews and the "seasons and events" of your prospect's and/or customer's year.

Here are examples:

- At the completion of your [bimonthly or quarterly] account reviews, you can say: *"Julia, are you happy with the performance of our 'star-wire' installation?"* *"Great. With that in mind, is there anyone that you might know who would benefit in a similar way from. . .?"*

- If you know that your prospect/customer attends an annual national conference, then you should prime the pump in this way: *"John, while you're at the national dry cleaners' convention this year, could you please do me a personal favor? Keep your eyes peeled for anyone that you think would have a need for [our chem-peel line of goods].*

- Talking to an Approver? After you broadcast the hard- and soft-dollar results they've been getting (or if this is a prospect, the results that await), say: *"Our mutual efforts have been well documented. And because of that, would you consider a personal favor on my behalf?"* (They will say something like this: *"What's on your mind?"*) You continue: *"Would you introduce me to someone who you know in the [niche/sister company/parent company/community, or whatever] who may be able to use my services to achieve similar or even greater results?"*

- Talking to a Decision Maker? After you broadcast the advantages of the hard- and soft-dollar results they've been getting (or if this is a prospect, the results that await), say: *"Would you be comfortable introducing me to someone of your equal line-of-business title at another organization here in Santa Barbara who may have an interest in what my organization has to offer?"*

- Talking to an Influencer? After you have established your credentials and credibility in your field, say: *"I trust that you see the unique differences in my product(s) and, to that end, I'd like to ask you if you would be willing to introduce me to someone you know who may be interested in our technical expertise."*

- Talking to a Recommender? After you have established that your ideas are relevant to this person's world, say: *"May I ask you to do me a favor?"* If they respond favorably or curiously, you continue with: *"Would you please introduce me to someone you know personally who I may be able to help in a similar way?"*

While You're on a Roll, Ask a Few Questions

As soon as you're given the name, I strongly suggest that you ask the following three questions:

1. "Could you tell me a little about [Mr. Bigshot]?" Then, you pick from the following questions:
   - "What is it about [Mr. Bigshot] that makes you feel that he would be interested in what I've got to offer?"
   - "Do you know what [product, service, or solution] he's currently using?"
   - "Can you tell me if [Mr. Bigshot] has any of the following goals or plans?" (Now you can mention several areas that you've got a track record in.)
   - "What can you tell me about [Mr. Bigshot's] personality style?"
   - "What's [Mr. Bigshot's] private assistant's name?"
   - "Does [Mr. Bigshot] have a private line?"
2. "Could you give [Mr. Bigshot] a call and let him know that I'll be calling him tomorrow at 9:30? (This one is a "seven pointer.") Important note: Always give a specific day and time that you'll be calling, and stick to it.
3. "Could you pick up the phone while I am here and introduce me to [Mr. Bigshot]?" (This one's a "ten pointer.")

Yes, people really will do this for you if you ask them to. I promise. It works.

Referral Guidelines

Here are some additional guidelines to follow in asking for referrals.

Existing Customers

When you stop to think about it, asking your existing customers for referrals is the lowest-hanging fruit you'll find. Apply what you've learned so far in this chapter, and pick your target.

Good: Ask your current customer contact (Recommender, Influencer, and/or Decision Maker) for a referral to someone of an equal or greater title in his or her organization or another organization (in your territory).

Better: Ask your current customer contact (Recommender, Influencer, and/or Decision Maker) to give their endorsement for your existing performance to the person to whom he or she reports, and request a meeting where all three of you can talk about how to duplicate the results elsewhere within the organization.

Best: Ask your current customer contact (Approver) to provide an endorsement for your existing performance to someone of equal title (another Approver, such as one of their board members) in another organization (in your territory) who may have similar needs.

Current Prospects

Don't fall for the old sales lie that you can't ask prospects for referrals. Of course you can.

The faster you can get your prospect familiar and pleased with you and your products, services, and solutions, the faster you'll get a referral. And the more prospects are pleased, the higher quality their referrals will be. The first step in getting to that point as quickly as possible is to have integrity. Simply put, do what you say you'll do, when you say you'll do it. That includes letting your prospects know as you approach them that your business and reputation is built on referrals, and that you'll be asking them as quickly as they feel comfortable doing so.

Good: Ask your current prospect to introduce you to someone she or he relies upon (suppliers, outsourcers, or an employee of a sister division) for any other major product, service, and/or solution that requires a similar or greater investment than what you sell.

Better: Ask your current prospect to introduce you to someone in her or his own company who may have a similar need for your products, services, and/or solutions.

Best: Ask your current prospect to introduce you to someone in an association or other professional organization (that she or he is active in) who would have a need for your products, services, and/or solutions.

A Word of Caution about Referral Reluctance

No matter how hard you try to prove yourself and your products, services, and solutions, some individuals will never feel comfortable providing the names of colleagues. Here are some of the reasons and what you can do about it.

- *They simply don't trust you.* This is a tough one to overcome, especially if you feel that you've done your part in the "you can trust me department." You can always try this:

  "Is there anything that I can do to make you feel more comfortable with providing me the names of your [colleagues, association members, Approver's name, or whatever]?"

- *They aren't clear about what you can offer.* This is a common problem with prospects. Asking for a referral before your prospect has a clear understanding of what you can and can't do won't help your referral cause or move you any closer to your No Cold-Calling model. The key here is not to get too anxious. Asking for a referral too soon will cause greater delays than necessary. You can hedge your bets here by testing the water for obtaining your referral. Try:

  "Let me leave you with this thought. Please don't keep me a secret. If there is someone you know who I might be able to help in a similar or even greater way, I'd love to have you introduce me to them in the very near future."

  The line, "Please don't keep me a secret," comes from my good friend Bill Cates, America's Number One Referral Coach.

- *They're concerned they'll hear someone say, "Why did you sic that salesperson on me?"* Try saying:

170

"If you like, you can call Suzanne and let her know I'll be calling. If she would feel more comfortable, perhaps we can do a three-way call or meet for coffee on Thursday morning."

- *They've already prequalified the person you want to be referred to and counted him or her out of your sales process.* Of all the referral reluctance issues you'll run into, this is the most serious. Your prospect is convinced that the individuals they know aren't going to be interested. Try saying this:

   "Julia, most of my prospects don't initiate a call to me because many of them don't realize that their time to market can be shortened without spending large amounts of capital monies. Would you be willing to ask Anthony if his production rework activity exceeds his last year's figures—so we can let him decide if what I can do is of interest to him?"

What's Next?

In the next chapter, you'll learn how to approach the people your contact refers you to.

Five Big Ideas

1. Be worthy of trust.

2. Set realistic expectations.

3. Document the payoff on the customer's investment.

4. Follow the Ten Commandments of referral generation.

5. Get over being afraid of asking. Just ask.

Don't forget to go to: www.stopcoldcalling.info for additional for-fee information. Click on "Chapter Fourteen: Online Assets."

NO COLD-CALLING
PRINCIPLE 15

"Ask and thou shalt receive. . .
What a concept!"

—E8486

CHAPTER FIFTEEN

Reaching Out

O CONGRATULATIONS! YOU GOT THAT PRECIOUS REFERRAL, THE ONE THAT'S going to make all the difference in your No Cold-Call Selling model and allow you to move toward that magic 40-in-100 ratio when it comes to setting a meeting. What's your approach?

Two Strategies

Here comes the fun part. There are two situations to plan for.

1. Your prospect and/or customer *is* willing to pick up the phone and make the introductory call.
2. Your prospect and/or customer *isn't* willing (or you didn't ask them— too bad) to pick up the phone and make the introductory call.

If you're lucky enough to find yourself in the first situation, you're golden. The majority of these situations will turn into face-to-face appointments. Follow up by phone, and request a meeting. Odds are, you'll get it.

Now let's look at the second scenario. Assume your contact doesn't want to make the call (or you didn't ask). You should send your new prospect a customized piece of correspondence (see Chapter Ten). You'll be "headlining" the fact that you have been referred to them.

In a letter:

- Make sure that you write on the outside of the envelope: "Ms. Bigshot suggested that I send you the enclosed information." (Of course, Ms. Bigshot is the person who gave you the referral.)
- Make sure the headline of your correspondence includes a testimonial that's written in the words and experiences of the prospect or customer who gave you the referral.
- If at all possible, include a testimonial letter (more on this in a moment).

In an e-mail message:

- Make sure that you put your prospect's or customer's name in the subject line: Topic: "Ms. Bigshot has asked me to contact you."
- Make sure that if you have a testimonial letter, you include it as an attachment.

In an e-presentation:

- If you can, include a slide with your prospect's or customer's voice on it speaking your praise.

Testimonial Letters

The power of the pen is, I believe, never as pragmatically expressed as in a well-written testimonial letter.

Offer to put together a first draft of the testimonial letter for your customer. (Nine times out of ten, the person will appreciate the offer and take you up on it.) Make sure the final draft of your testimonial letter includes:

- Specific results that you've accomplished, stated in terms of hard/tangible or soft/intangible results (as described in several chapters in this book).
- The specific period of time it took your customer to realize his or her own ROI.

Of course, many a salesperson will tell you that getting effective testimonial letters is nearly impossible. Here again, we must be willing to come to terms with our own self-limiting beliefs. If we do just a little digging, we will find that our best customers are more than happy to sing our praises. All we have to do is follow the lead of what may well be the best business quote of all time, from a global bestseller I'm sure you have it around the house: "Ask and thou shalt receive."

- Some small chart or verbiage that can show the before vs. the after impact that your product, service, or solution has created.
- The title of the person who authored the letter.
- The logo of the company giving you the testimonial. (It's best to get the entire letter on its company stationery.)

Keep 'em Posted

Warning: Your job isn't done just because you asked for and received a referral. It's not done when you call and introduce yourself to that person. And it's not done when you get the meeting.

You owe it to your referral source to close the loop. A simple e-mail or voice mail letting the person who gave you the name know what happened will suffice. Tell your contact that you have called the person in question, and briefly explain what happened on that call.

That's not all. Whether or not you make a sale, you might want to think seriously about thanking your referring contact in a special way.

Yeah, yeah, I know. You already send so many thank-you notes you can hardly keep track of them all. All I'm saying is that you should make sure you send a special note or other form of recognition to your referral sources. Do it on the same day you get the referral, *not* the day you make contact.

Four Big Ideas

1. First, try to get the person giving you the referral to make an introductory call on your behalf.

2. If he or she is unwilling to do so, be ready to write a piece of customized correspondence yourself, one that prominently features the referring contact's name in its headline.

3. Use a testimonial letter. Customers are more willing to authorize one than you think. Offer to write the first draft.

4. Write a thank-you letter to the referring contact the day you receive the referral.

We're heading for the barn. Turn the page, and dive headfirst into the last chapter.

Don't forget to go to: www.stopcoldcalling.info for additional for-fee information on this chapter that will assist you in creating testimonial letters and other related materials. Click on "Chapter Fifteen: Online Assets."

Notes

Notes

NO COLD-CALLING
PRINCIPLE 16

"The object of an objection

is to sell past it."

—E8486

The Last Frontier

HIS IS THE LAST CHAPTER FOR ME—THE END OF THIS BOOK. AND IT'S THE beginning for you.

I want to assure you that it will be necessary for you to approach everything you've learned in the book—and the simple principles that appear in this chapter—with a determined mindset. One that says, "I am unstoppable, I am unflappable, and I am totally committed in my desire to rid myself of cold calling forever."

Objections

In this chapter I'll show you how to tackle every single, possible objection that has ever come your way and perhaps a few that you haven't encountered yet. What you're about to experience in this last chapter will go against what you've learned in the past. Use it—because what you have been using up to this point is not working for you today.

These are my personal secrets for dealing with bumps along the road to warm calls and turning them into opportunity. What you're going to read is how I do my sales work. As Ol' Blue Eyes put it, this is "my way."

Uncle Frankie

No, Sinatra wasn't my uncle, but I did have an Uncle Frankie. I grew up in Hoboken, New Jersey. So did Frank Sinatra. *My* Uncle Frankie was one of the most important and influential teachers in my life. He named his beautiful 26-foot cabin cruiser after his favorite Sinatra song, "My Way."

This part of the book is dedicated to my Uncle Frankie. It's where you will learn about My Way to select, engage, listen, and launch—My Way to SELL. My Way to be a consistent top producer and win every award, trophy, and contest in the world of selling. My Way for you to make so much money that your main problem will be finding worthy causes to give it to.

This is the part of the book where I invite you to make My Way *your* way. In the end, you'll thank me, my Uncle Frankie, and, yeah, maybe even that other Frankie.

SELL: Select, Engage, Launch, Listen
Step 1: Select
The first part of our countdown is to do some "preflight" work by selecting which prospects you'll be calling on.

A TIP for Success
Did you know that the word *Tip*—as in "to leave a tip for a waiter"—stands for "To Insure Performance"? That's right. In the old days, whenever travelers would give money in advance of getting a service (like bedding down their weary horses for the night after a long day's ride), this advance to the stable keeper would guarantee their horses' needs would be met.

If you doubt the power of this principle, try this little experiment. Next time you're in Las Vegas and you're standing in line to be seated at a show, as the maître d' takes your ticket, hand him a $20 bill. Whoosh. Guess what? If it is open seating, you're in one of the best seats in the house.

Do you think the strategy would work as well if you said to the maître d', "Give me a good seat, and I'll give you a nice tip on the way out"?

A TIP really does work better if it's done in advance to insure performance. Early in this book, I spent a great deal of time emphasizing that if you want to find the best individuals and organizations in your sales territory, you'll use a Template of Ideal Prospects *before* you make contact.

Selling the Hard Way Means. . .

Ignoring what I said about the TIP. Then beating a dead horse. Then beating your head against a hard surface. Then going absolutely nuts calling anyone and everyone you *think* could be a good prospect. It means enduring the rejection rate of a salesperson selling ice to Eskimos or screen doors to the United States Navy submarine fleet.

Selling "My Way" Means. . .

Following my advice about the TIP. Entering the world of prospects who are predisposed to work with you. Only calling on individuals and organizations that are a perfect fit to your business. (No exceptions.) It means making the cold call a thing of the past and selling at a level you never dreamed possible.

I have nine parameters that my prospects must measure up to, parameters that are specific to my business. If a company doesn't match all nine, I won't contact them. Period. I do not make any exceptions to this rule. At first, I was concerned. Heck, I was downright terrified that I wouldn't have enough activity in my sales funnel if I followed this rule. But I followed it anyway. And guess what? I was wrong. I had *plenty* of people to talk to.

There are tons of prospects that fit your TIP in your territory. Ignore all temptation to settle for anything less than prospects that are a *perfect* fit to you and your products, services, and solutions. These are individuals who are predisposed to buying from you.

Go back to Chapter One, and ingest it. Do your work, and join in on the fun of taking shortcuts to every person and organization that's predisposed to buying from you.

Step 2: Engage

If you're going to make a splash, why not make it a really big one? Here again My Way kicks in big time. I hate wasting anything, especially time. Oh, I haven't always had this attitude. When I was 19, two years seemed like a lifetime. Now I find that two years is a virtual eye blink. Time is passing at an alarming rate. And that's why we (you and I) need to make the best of it.

I talked earlier about creating buzz in and around your products, services, and solutions with as many different media outlets as you can find. And we dove headfirst into what I call the fab four: the functions, features, advantages, and benefits that are tied, respectively, to Recommenders, Influencers, Decision Makers, and Approvers.

So here's the gig. You and I must create our own media. We are the best presenters of whatever it is that we are selling. We must locate and contact "local" media, whether it's radio, TV, and/or print. And at the same time, we need to engage the *right* individual within your base of TIP prospects. Who's the right individual?

Selling the Hard Way Means. . .

Sell like a king. (A King Salmon, that is.) Ever watch a King Salmon in its yearly migratory trek? This is what they pass on to their young: Put in all the effort and energy to swim upriver and die. Not a pretty sight.

Now, I admit Mother Nature is beautiful, but that's not a great metaphor for sales mastery.

Ask yourself: How many times have you found yourself putting in the effort and energy to get a sale? Pushing and pushing, jumping through hoop after hoop, only to watch your sale die a slow and painful death—all because you started with the wrong person, someone you thought was easy to get to but who then blocked you and your sales efforts? Ouch.

Selling "My Way" Means. . .

Start high and go low. Remember that benefits are business-centric, not product- or customer-centric. That simple fact will help you engage the right person in every prospect organization that fits your TIP.

Who's the right person? When in doubt, head for the top, and make contact with the Approver of your sale. How do you know who that is? Simple. Pick the biggest, loftiest, highest-titled person in each organization that fits your TIP. Bingo, you've got the Approver. Now create your *benefit*, your business-centric statement, and you'll be ready to tackle the launching of your No Cold-Calling sales model.

Picture a telephone pole, and ask yourself this question: How many tops does it have? One. That's the Approver; Approvers sit at the top. And one thing about the top—there's only one seat.

If you've got the choice (and you usually will), that's who you'll engage with first.

Step 3: Launch

Remember the wave? Catch it, or wipe out.

There is no way that you'll eliminate cold calling from your sales work if you're not willing to put together a wave that *precedes* your contacting those *predisposed* prospects that fit your TIP to a T. In Chapter Eleven, I gave you five different combinations to facilitate this wave. Each required that you put together a correspondence by following a particular format (see Chapter Nine and Ten). Each of these combos had three to four pieces to it. Its power is unleashed prior to your making contact, and it sets the stage for what follows.

Don't skip the setting-the-stage part.

Selling the Hard Way

Keep doing what you're doing. Keep getting so little from your prospecting efforts that you give up on making the effort because it's "just a waste of time." Keep shot-gunning your territory, cold calling to create just enough activity to keep your sales manager off your back. If that assessment hurts, guess what? It's true.

Selling "My Way"

Call it a "squeeze play" on multiple contacts. It's an advanced maneuver, but it's something you can work your way up to. Here's what I do.

- I send the Approver a postcard telling her or him to be on the lookout for an e-presentation on a certain day and date. (More on this in a minute.)
- Then as promised, I send the e-presentation. On the same date that I sent the postcard, I'll initiate contact with the person the Decision Maker depends upon (the Influencer) for input on my particular services, the head of the organization's training department. I send a piece of correspondence accompanied by a sample of my work

(typically a book and an audio program, and/or a video program). I do this because I know that, typically, Influencer's love stuff.

- On the third business day after I've taken Steps 1 and 2, I pick up the telephone (after hours) and call the Decision Maker (typically, the vice president of sales), leaving a voice-mail message:

  "In the next few days your president may give you a call about me and an idea that I have for your sales team. And it's possible that the head of your training department may stop by and want to talk to you about Selling to VITO. *If you'd like to know more, you can reach me at 1-800-777-8486. Oh, almost forgot, my name is Tony, Tony Parinello. The best time to reach me is between 3:00 and 6:00 P.M. Tuesday, Wednesday, or Thursday of this week. Have a great rest of the day, and I look forward to hearing from you."*

Here's a challenge. Do it My Way for just two months, and see what your numbers look like.

Put together your postcard. Do some research. Get the names of the Approver, Decision Maker, and typical Influencer of your sale from a prospect that fits your TIP. Then push the launch button.

By the way, wanna see a dynamite e-presentation? I thought so. Just go to: www.stopcoldcalling.info, and click on "Chapter Sixteen: Online Assets."

Step 4: Listen

Hear what your prospects say—and in some cases, don't say.

I recently saw a T-shirt that had beautiful, brightly colored gold letters on it. In large print it simply said: *It's All About Me.*

> What I want to do here is teach you how to use listening skills to handle *all* of the initial objections you'll be hearing from your prospects as you make your telephone or in-person calls. Truth be told, when it comes to selling, there will always be objections. The way you handle them will prove to your prospects how good a listener you really are or aren't.

Picture every single prospect who fits your TIP wearing a T-shirt that bears that message. It really is all about them.

If you need a tune-up on your listening skills, check out the nation's leading expert on the topic of listening, Madelyn Burley-Allen. Her work is epic.

Playing It Cool

If you're passionate about what you do for a living—and I hope you are—you're going to have to make a determined effort to maintain your composure when a prospect starts launching objections about your product, service, or solution. It's natural, to some degree, to take these remarks personally, but it's also essential to keep your sense of balance and perspective when you're feeling you're on the grill.

> Don't shoot from the hip. Don't improvise. Don't panic. Follow these simple rules when a prospect tells you your specs aren't right, your price is too high, your reputation isn't good enough, or your quality is suspect.

Rule 1: Remember, Everything Your Prospect Says Has Face Value.
Don't fight (internally or externally) with the individual who passed along the objection. Don't rebut. Don't get into point-by-point struggles. Take what follows to heart when you answer any objection.

Rule 2: Compare the Objection to Your Own History as a Salesperson.
Is this objection something that, historically, you have had no control over? Is it unique to this buyer? Odds are, this objection has something in common with one you've heard before. Ask yourself, "Have I ever sold to someone who told me this?"

Rule 3: Analyze the Objection.
Is it reasonable? Would you make this objection if you were in your prospect's shoes?

Rule 4: Look at the Big Picture Before You Respond.

Remember, you don't have to sell every person you come in contact with to be ahead of quota. You just have to sell the right ones.

Rule 5: Never Offer Judgments Concerning the Validity of the Objection.

Instead learn how to question the objection.

See What They Say

After years and years of hearing objections, I reached the following conclusions.

First, I had to totally disregard the standard "objection handlers" I found in sales books, such as "I understand how you feel; others have felt that way. Blah, blah, blah." None of it worked as well as I needed it to.

Second, there were really only two general ways to address what is at the heart of every objection. The first way I did this was by actually seeing what my prospects were saying, and the second way was to put words in their mouths. That sounds weird or even manipulative, but it's neither. Read on.

What follows are seven easy ways to see past the objection and one really cool way to introduce an objection before your prospect does.

Objection Strategy 1: Up the Ante

When you question the objection tactfully and politely, you call the prospect's bid and raise her or him one. This approach is dramatic, and it's not what you'll read about in most sales training books. But I know you'll find that it delivers some extraordinary results if you do it—and stick with it.

Questioning the objection allows you to get to the bottom of things in a hurry, which is what My Way is all about. After all, if there really is an insurmountable objection, don't you want to find out about it as soon as possible and track down prospects who are likelier to do business with you? Good, I thought so.

Questioning the objection involves using an "If not, then what?" formula. Here's an example of how questioning the objection works in practice:

> *Prospect*: "Thanks for showing me the fall line, but your wholesale price is just too high. After we apply our standard markup, the retail

price would be too high for the clientele who shop in our discount chain. I'll pass."

You: "Hmm. OK, if our price were lower, low enough for you to make margin and price it right for your outlets, would you place an order for your stores today?"

Prospect: (Surprised pause, then) "No, the problem is that the style and material really aren't what I think they ought to be."

Bingo! Price wasn't the insurmountable obstacle you'd been led to believe. You're perfectly positioned to show other merchandise to this buyer.

You can use this tactic with virtually any objection that could come your way.

Here's another example that shows you how to put the spotlight on the real sales opportunity:

Prospect: "The price you're charging for your seminar on May 14 is just too high. I can't afford it."

Top Salesperson (i.e., You): "That's interesting. If the seminar were free, would you want to attend?"

Prospect: (After a long pause) "Well, to tell you the truth, no, I wouldn't. See, the problem is that I don't really like to be stuffed in some conference room with a bunch of my competitors, all learning the same thing."

Top Salesperson: "Here, take a look at this. A complete online success kit that includes workbooks, MP3 downloads, and tons of additional information you can't get at the live event—all with unlimited access.

> Don't offer to lower your price. Lowering your price will only lower your profit margins and drive you out of business. Stop the madness. Don't take the bait. Don't ask your company to lower its prices to satisfy price-shopping prospects.

And it's all at a fraction of the price of the seminar. More importantly, it comes with a success coach for one-on-one mentoring."

While we're on the subject of price. . .

Objection Strategy 2: The Price Is Right

At my seminars I'll ask the audience, "Who here is working on a deal where they're getting beat up on price?" Consistently, 30 to 50 percent of the audience will raise their hands. That's a ridiculously high number, wouldn't you say?

You know what I think? I think it's a setup. Your prospects know that you're desperate to make the sale. And they also know that, all else being equal, the only meaningful negotiating point will be price. Try this:

Prospect: "Your price is too high." (Or: "You have a reputation of being the higher-priced provider.")

Top Salesperson: "Please define price."

Wow! Now your prospect is on the spot to articulate what price means to him or her—and you're in a position to listen and learn.

Don't ask a stupid question, one that will give you an answer that you can't do anything with. For example:

- "Just how much too high is our price?"
- "How much lower does my price need to be?"
- "What price are you willing to spend?"

Know exactly what your limitations are and how much room you have to lower your price, and knock it down before anyone asks you to do it. Or better yet, keep your prices high, and sell only to prospects who appreciate the indisputable fact that you'll always get what you pay for.

Objection Strategy 3: Shed a Little Light

The toughest objections are probably the ones where your prospect gives you little or no information to work with. In many cases, of course, you'll be looking at a dead end. But there are ways you can make drama and enthusiasm work for you in these settings. Say you're talking to a Decision Maker and he or she says something like this:

"Thanks for your offer, but I simply have no interest whatsoever."

One flamboyant way to get back on the saddle is to pose a "what if" question along the following lines. (Note that the question is keyed to a positive result closely associated with a direct concern of this Decision Maker.)

Top Salesperson: "Ms. Manager, if the person you trust the most to lower the cost of your long-distance bills were to walk into your office with this idea, would you be interested in looking into it further?"

If your Decision Maker prospect says "No," say "thank you" and hang up. File that call under "Hey, it takes some no answers to get to a yes." But suppose you hear your prospect say something like:

Prospect: "Well, maybe I would give it some thought."

Guess what? You're in business. End the call pleasantly. Check with the reception desk, and find out who's in charge of long-distance service (or whatever you discussed with the Decision Maker). Call that person up, and say:

Top Salesperson: "I just hung up with Ms. Manager. She told me that if you were to bring this idea to her attention, she would take a look at it. Here's the idea—tell me what you think."

I've interviewed thousands of prospects who fall into the Decision Maker and Approver category. You know what I've learned? They're constantly testing us. Why? Because they only want to buy from the best salespeople around.

Become the Best Damned Salesperson in the World

Here's the point: The easiest way to fail the test is to put your tail between your legs and run whenever you hear what appears to be an insurmountable objection.

Look at it this way: You're on a job interview whenever an objection comes your way. If your prospect would hire you, they'll do business with you.

Objection Strategy 4: Take the Challenge

Let's say for a moment that your prospect is extremely happy with whomever the current source of supply is—so happy, in fact, that he or she would never, ever consider switching. That is, until you show up.

Prospect: "I saw your e-mail. Thanks for the call, but I am all set. My current P.R. firm is taking care of all my brand-awareness needs."

Top Salesperson: "Before you hang up, let me ask you—would you like to know what your loyalty to your current P.R. firm is costing you?"

I strongly suggest you use this verbatim. It's a very powerful way to find out if there is any shred of interest. And it's also a direct, but appropriate, challenge to the prospect's position. This is powerful stuff.

Bottom line: If you hear anything other than a click and a dial tone, you're in. Take a look:

Prospect: "What do you mean by that?"

Top Salesperson: "The other customers we have in your industry tell me that they're now able to _____." (Fill in the blank with every single aspect of your Product Value Inventory we discussed in Chapter Four that you know you deliver and your competition doesn't.)

This response also works well for any prospects who have an internal source of supply that they're "totally" satisfied with. For example, if your prospect says, "My P.R. department is taking care of all of my needs," your response would be the same.

Don't turn and run when you hear this objection. This supposed deal-breaker sends many a salesperson away, feeling rejected and questioning whether or not they should go back to school and get yet another degree so they can get a "real" job. Don't you be one of them.

I promise you, you *will* earn the respect of your prospect if you do use this approach and stand firm.

Be prepared. Have your response at the ready; rehearse it with your sales manager or a peer that you respect. Get your ducks in a row. Know the real differentiators between you and your closest competition.

Objection Strategy 5: Been There, Done That, Got the T-Shirt

Just about every company in existence has had some problem account that they really messed up and, as a result, have lost. Then along comes a new, unsuspecting salesperson in the territory—or maybe the past messed-up customer turns up on a hot-prospect list. Here's what it sounds like:

Prospect: "We used your line of [detergent], and it cost us a fortune in repair bills for our steam washers. I'll never use your company again."

Top Salesperson: "Sorry to hear that. Let me ask you, if your company's best salesperson just heard that objection from one of their past customers, how would you personally coach them in answering it?"

If you hear anything other than a click and a dial tone, you're in business. Suppose you hear something like this:

Prospect: "I'd tell your production department to get a new formula, and then I'd tell your quality assurance department to put proper warning labels on your packaging. And I'd tell your sales department to know everything about their product *before* they go out and try to sell it." Etc., etc., etc.

As this prospect dumps on you, make sure you take notes. When the person is all done and feels heard, you can say something.

Top Salesperson: "Thank you very much. Here's what we've done. (Now articulate what, if anything, you've done to correct the situation—and more importantly, what you've done that *this* prospect suggested be done.)

The biggest insult you can give any prospect at this point is to become a "parrot" and say something totally lame:

Lousy Salesperson: "I can see that you've had a bad experience with our company in the past. Well, fortunately, that salesperson is no longer here. I am committed to doing whatever it takes to win your business back. Blah, blah, blah. . ."

This will only succeed in getting the other person to tune out.

Be an ambassador for your organization, take the heat, do whatever it takes to make it right, and see to it that you and whatever you're selling are engaged in a constant improvement program.

Objection Strategy 6: Really *Send Some Information*

If you're selling commercial printing services, I apologize in advance. You're not going to like what you're about to read.

Sending information to your prospects is a waste of time.

Prospect: "I saw the postcard you sent me. I'm interested, so why don't you send me some information."

Top Salesperson: "I'd be glad to. We've got a documentation package that will answer any question you might have about our superior line of products. It's quite big, weighing 175 pounds and standing 6'2" inches tall. We call it Tony. When would you like it to arrive at your place?"

Don't do this:

Lousy Salesperson: "OK, give me your address."

We're running out of public landfills at an alarming rate because sales-people continue to send information to prospects who really aren't inter-ested. (Some folks really do want information, of course; in fact, they're on a quest to collect as much information as they possibly can—information they can give to their incumbent provider.)

As a general rule, you should never, ever send information to any prospect until you've qualified their needs. And if at all possible, you should hand-carry any information to your prospect, so you can discuss it during your first in-person meeting.

Objection Strategy 7: Don't Agree to "Call Me in Two Months from Never"

You sent the e-presentation, you call to follow up, and everything's going great. Your prospect seems interested enough, but he's preoccupied. He makes a request that you've heard a thousand times before:

Prospect: "I am interested in your line of crop dusters, but I've got to do some year-end budget planning first. Call me in three months."

(What to do? Take a look.)

Top Salesperson: "Sure. Let me ask you, though: Let's say it's three months from now. What exactly would you want to see, hear, or expe-rience during that time that would provide a complete understanding of our products, services, and solutions?"

Prospect: "Well, I'd first want to talk to someone who has a similar need to mine, then I'd want to take a ride in the crop duster, and finally I'd want to have my aviation director take a look."

Top Salesperson: "I've got an idea. How about you and I grab a bite to eat with one of my customers sometime in the next month? What's your calendar look like?"

Or: "How about this? While you're crunching numbers, I can have a conversation with your director of aviation about. . ."

The key here is to offer several suggestions as to steps and actions that can easily take place during the idle time the prospect suggested.

It never ceases to amaze me how many salespeople will obediently take the blow-off and actually agree to give a callback in three months from never. Make no mistake, during that time your competition will be calling on this prospect and outposition you in the interim.

Have an arsenal of information, tactics, activities, correspondence, newsletters, touch points, lunches, lattes, and so forth that you can offer in response to the endless blow-off. It beats knee-jerk acceptance of a blow-off.

Objection Strategy 8: The Best Offense Is a Good Defense

This extremely cool, highly effective, unorthodox strategy for dealing with objections comes to you courtesy of Joe Sugarman, the king of infomercials and an icon in marketing. You may not recognize his name, but you most likely have one or more of his products, such as his blue-blocker sunglasses. Here then is one of the best sales tactics that I've ever learned, compliments of Mr. Sugarman.

Every single product, service, and solution in existence has its fair share of flaws. So the question is, what are you as a salesperson going to do when those flaws are pointed out? Oh, sure, you could be on the defense and "handle" the problem when it comes up, but how about turning the table? How about bringing up your worse objection before your prospect does? How about bringing it up when you want to talk about it?

Let me give you an example. Let's say you're selling the highest-priced chemical cleaner on the market. And let's say that the price objection always rears its ugly head at a time when it typically isn't favorable to closing the sale that you've worked on so hard.

Top Salesperson (You): "Mr. Lowball, you'll find that we're the only provider of high-quality, extended-shelf-life, and EPA-compliant chemical cleaners on the market. And you'll also find that we're the highest-priced solution."

(There. You came right out and said it.)

Prospect: "Well, that's a problem. I've been asked to reduce expenses for the balance of this year."

Smart Salesperson: "Have you completed your annual EPA inspection?"

Prospect: "No, it's due to start in the third quarter."

Smart Salesperson: "Shall we provide you with enough cleaner to satisfy your needs until the end of the third quarter—and guarantee that you pass the inspection with flying colors?"

In every single case you'll gain the respect and confidence of your prospect with this approach.

Warning: Don't just throw any old objection out there in a lame attempt to get your prospect's attention. Doing so will backfire and be seen by your prospect as a smoke screen to possibly cover up a more serious and unspoken problem. Result? You'll lose what little credibility you didn't have.

Congratulations

Take your left hand, place it on your right shoulder, and give yourself a pat on the back.

You've reached the end of this book and the beginning of a cold-calling-free life in Sales Heaven. Don't forget to access the online for-fee assets at the end of some chapters. If you find yourself stuck on any issue regarding our wonderful profession of sales, point your Internet browser toward my weekly talk show, "Selling Across America" (www.sellingacrossamerica. com). It's dedicated to salespeople. You'll find me there each and every Friday, live. Or catch me whenever you want by listening to my archives.

Here's to your massively beautiful success in sales!

Afterword

I HOPE YOU ENJOYED MY TONGUE-IN-CHEEK STORY IN THE FOREWORD ABOUT how I met Tony. Actually, I have had the privilege of being Tony's personal success coach and longtime friend. He and I have enjoyed working together to mentor over 1 million sales professionals across America, and it has truly been a pleasure to contribute to the ongoing success of his alumni.

As I see it, you have the opportunity to use the information in this book in one of two ways:

1. As a form of entertainment.
2. To prepare for Peak Performance in your sales career.

I'll assume you've selected Option 2. I assume, too, that you've read every word and took the time to go online and get all of the additional information that Tony offered you. Now you must be determined to take *ACTION!*

If you look back on anything you have ever accomplished in life you'll find a common and simple truth. You took action. You weren't a spectator, and you didn't sit around observing someone else—you were in the game.

You were right in the middle of the experience, offering up your heart and soul. You gave it your all.

In several places in this book, Tony asked you to do pick-and-shovel work. Did you do it? Did you get into the game? This is critical to the value that you get from this book and the way you operate as a sales professional.

If you're on the fence and in need of a push to get you started, I invite you to read the following two appendixes. The first one is written by me and is my gift to you. It will help you with critical success strategies and your efforts to put Tony's ideas and strategies to work. The second appendix written by Dr. Kathleen Brooks, one of the nation's leading authorities on how self-development helps overcome fear.

I just heard "batter up" from the umpire. Knock it out of the park!

—Steve Dailey

Success Tracks:
Meet Steve Dailey

S TEVE HAS BEEN A PERSONAL SUCCESS COACH FOR THE LAST 26 YEARS. HE started his first business with less than $200 and shaped it into a multimillion-dollar organization in just three years. In other words, Steve is no armchair strategist. He's a doer, the founder of Prime Focus, Inc., a coaching and consulting enterprise that serves entrepreneurs, business executives, and sales professionals in a multitude of business models and marketplaces. If you like, you can contact Steve directly at: sdailey@ primefocuscoaching.com.

Obstacles to Success

Let's get right to the point. As a professional coach, I have observed several traits that stand in the way of ultimate achievement and success in sales.

- Most salespeople are fast starters and poor finishers.
- Most salespeople are long on ambition and short on endurance.
- Most salespeople completely underestimate their potential.
- Most salespeople miss big opportunities every day.

Are any of these you?

Four Power Strategies

If you are any of these salespeople, let me help coach you through Four Power Strategies that have the potential to completely change your future. This will be brief and to the point. Have a pencil, paper, and your calendar handy, and do your best to open your mind to some new ideas—one more time. *What you are about to learn will add exponential value to Tony's remarkable insights.*

Power Strategy 1: Use the Right Information to Predict Your Future.

In the chapters you just read, Tony encouraged you to let go of the "mind chatter" that might cause you to predict that what he was suggesting wouldn't work.

Here's the deal: *Belief is a choice.* You can either believe something will work, or you can believe that it won't. But because you don't know what is going to happen anyway, why not choose to believe in what you want?

It always amazes me how people I coach will automatically predict their *future* on the basis of what happened in the *past*. The past is the wrong information to look at. In the past, you were a different person. You weren't as smart as you are today. You weren't as old as you are today. The circumstances around you were not the same as they are today. Yesterday is old, virtually irrelevant information. Today—and specifically what you decide to *believe* today—has a much greater impact on where you end up than anything that you might have experienced before today.

So how does that relate to selling? Selling *today* requires new ideas, new techniques, and new beliefs. What worked yesterday or didn't work yesterday has nothing to do with it. Tony has just dispensed real-world, thought-leading ideas that can revolutionize your selling power. Predict your future success by deciding to believe it *can* work, then deciding to believe it *will* work.

Use this one strategy today. Formulate your beliefs to support where you want to go instead of where you've been. You'll find yourself following through like never before, instead of stopping before you really got started, because you were looking at the wrong information.

Power Strategy 2: If It Ain't Important, Don't Do It.

How much of your productive workday have you spent on things that directly impact your sales success—selling quota, numbers on the board, closed deals? You know—money in your pocket. Be honest. Is it 60 percent, 50 percent, 20 percent, less?

I call it "presentee-ism." It's like "absenteeism" except you are there and just not doing anything. Most salespeople I coach determine at some point that in order to truly meet their potential, they have to *stop wasting time.* For some psychological reason, human beings have a tendency to gravitate to those activities (particularly during a workday) that have absolutely nothing to do with the production that is most important to them. There are always plenty of tasks, details, minutia, and tiddlywinks that have absolutely nothing to do with money in your pocket, but seductively lure your attention.

If you sincerely want to find out what your earning and success potential is—if you really want to improve your endurance and stop spending time on stuff that doesn't matter—stop right now and analyze every single thing you do during a workday. If it is not directly contributing to your selling success, do everything in your power to run from it, hide it, delegate it, lose it, forget about it, destroy it. If it ain't important, don't do it.

Power Strategy 3: Determine to Be Good at Everything So That You Can Be Extraordinary at One Thing.

Up until now, you may have gotten away with making your numbers or making a good income on the basis of relying on a particularly good skill or attribute. Maybe you are a great relationship person, and people buy from you because they like you. Maybe you are terrific at getting your production group to rush jobs so that you always look like a hero to your customers. Or maybe you do a great job at getting Recommenders and Influencers on your side in the sales process.

Whatever you are good at, in today's selling world, it isn't good enough.

The fact is that in order to be exceptional at any one thing—like closing deals consistently—you have to be at least good at everything. You have to be good at every single sales competency you can name, or you will wake up one day consistently getting beat. That's how it is in the marketplace today.

Before you decide you want to go back to work as a waiter and quit the selling game, let me put your mind at ease. The number of sales professionals honestly willing to develop and get good at all the required skills of selling in order to be truly exceptional in one area is very, very small. Don't kid yourself. Everyone is getting better all the time. But as a rule, no one is really looking at the whole picture as you are capable of doing now that you've read Tony's book.

Most salespeople are trying to skate along on the good graces of that one skill or trait that has always come through for them. It's not enough!

Change. Become at least good at everything so that you can become exceptional in at least one thing. Like cold calling.

Power Strategy 4: Use Your Pockets.

Here's the key to absolutely exploding your sales potential: Use all your pockets.

Let me explain. You know how your jeans have a whole bunch of pockets, but you really only use one or two? Over time, we all get used to using just one or two pockets. We only carry a certain amount of junk in our pockets (if anything). We put our hands in our pockets out of boredom, and we hardly ever think about how our pockets can be resources, instead of decoration.

What are the pockets in your selling profession?

Time

There are pockets of time that you can use, perhaps only 10 or 20 minutes at a time—but dozens of pockets in a week. If you truly used them well you could apply the time to a certain purpose. Don't put your hands in your pockets out of boredom and read the paper or smoke a cigarette. Do one of Tony's exercises or techniques every chance you get. Make an unscheduled call to a loyal customer to say "thank you," and get a testimonial for your next fax message to prospects. Corner your boss to ask him or her what they think is the hottest marketplace opportunity. Tune in to SellingAcrossAmerica.com to catch an archived segment of a sales legend.

People

People are pockets of resources. Who do you know who knows more than you about selling, about your market, or about your products? Bosses, sales peers, the folks over in manufacturing, the team in accounting—there are pockets of people right under your nose that can make you smarter and more agile in your business. If you don't find out how big or useful those pockets of people are, you're missing the boat. How about pockets of prospects like those at trade shows, user groups, seminars, networking meetings, and so on? Check out those pockets, and you'll be amazed at their capacity and potential.

Money

You have pockets of money that go unused, unnoticed, or underutilized. You used a pocket of money perhaps to buy this book. What other books, tapes, seminars, or workshops might enhance your professional expertise? Tap into a pocket of money for personal and professional development, and you'll find greater wealth. Guaranteed.

Success

So there they are, four fabulous success strategies to add power and velocity to your selling efforts and ignite your application of the ideas that you learned in earlier chapters of this book.

But there's one more suggestion I have for you. Every successful professional, in selling or in any area, that I have seen reach the top of their field has a personal success coach. If you want to find a coach who's a perfect fit for you and your goals, I'd love to hear from you.

Great success to you.

(By the way, if you haven't read everything in this book and completed all the exercises, I strongly suggest that you do it now.)

Facing Fear:
Meet Dr. Kathleen Brooks

OR THE LAST 25 YEARS, KATHLEEN HAS SPECIALIZED IN INTEGRATING PSYCHO-logical and spiritual growth through her consulting and mediation services with organizations such as Chase Manhattan Bank, monthly workshops titled "Awakening Awareness," weekly Internet talk show "Ethics from the Bedroom to the Boardroom," and her most recent book *Radical Integrity, 21 Ways to Create a Meaningful Life*. Kathleen has degrees in music and education and a Ph.D. in psychology. She has been an educator since 1961, facilitated trainings for teachers and business professionals, facilitated parent groups, and run a program for gifted junior high students. You can contact Kathleen directly at: www.ethicalife.com.

Making Fear an Ally

Fear is a tough one! Dealing successfully with the world in general—and specifically selling—requires that we make "friends" with fear. I call it *making an ally of fear*. If we don't do this, fear chases us around, and we end up at its mercy. Not a good way to live and certainly not a good way to sell. Whatever you do, stop running from fear.

In order to make fear into an ally instead of the enemy, it seems to many of us that the first thing we need to understand is what emotions are and how they work. There are really just two basic emotions, although they come with lots of variations and intensities: One set is caused by *pain*, and the other by *pleasure*.

The emotions caused by pleasure are the ones we like and seek out. What makes me feel good? That's what I want to have more of. We all love feeling happy, being "up." In fact, we learn to comfort ourselves when we feel bad by finding something that eases the pain, something that feels good. Did you suck your thumb as a baby? Smart way to comfort yourself when Momma wasn't around. Our efforts to find pleasure for ourselves are endless and quite brilliant.

As to what makes me feel bad, get me away. We don't want to feel bad because it hurts. In fact, fear is actually the warning that comes up around pain; it registers as a powerful body sensation that gets our attention. Watch out! This is going to hurt. (It may be real. It may not. But it sure looks that way.) You could say that fear is nothing but the discomfort about possible pain, accompanied by a strong motivation to avoid whatever seems to be the source of the pain (like keeping busy instead of making prospecting calls). This is a natural occurrence with humans, and we pretty much all do it instinctively. In fact, it's one of the earliest skills we acquire. Why did we decide to lie to our parents at some point? (Oh come on, you know you did.) Simple. We figured out the things they were going to punish us for if we got caught doing them. We're no dummies.

The problem with fear is that sometimes we really are in danger and we really are going to get hurt, but sometimes we're not. So before we can learn how to make fear an ally, we've got to have a way to identify whether it's a *real* fear or an *imagined* one. This is called doing a reality check. Chances are, if the fear is real, you're already in action. You will do the perfect thing—survive as best you can. It's the fears that aren't real that are the problem. After all, it's a terrific waste of energy to go around fighting phantoms.

How do you differentiate between emotions and feelings? They're actually two different situations. Emotions occur as strong physical sensations accompanied by the immediate desire to be in action. They are the most accurate indicator you have about how things look to you and how they are affecting you. It's pretty simple. *Emotions are real reactions to a real situation that is actually happening right now.* An example is the natural, real emotion that arises if and when we experience being in the middle of an earthquake. Yup, we're scared all right. We don't stop to wonder if we're *imagining* the earth opening up underneath. We're feeling the earth move, and we're looking down into the chasm. Furthermore, we aren't likely to go into a long rumination, filing through a list of options that might work. We just move our butts real fast. It all happens quickly and without much thought. That's emotion.

Feelings, on the other hand, are physical sensations accompanied by the desire to be in action, and are caused not by what's actually going on, but by how it looks to us. Feelings originate from a memory of being in a similar situation that had a certain outcome that caused emotions. *Feelings come from imagined situations rather than real ones.* A simple example is the feeling of being hurt when someone makes a comment to us that we hear as an insult (like feeling rejected by a receptionist). They may or may not have meant to insult us. (They're just doing their job by directing us to the right person.) They may have been making what they thought was the right decision. On the other hand, we imagined they were rejecting us. Those are feelings.

Why do we want to know the difference between feelings and emotions? Because when we react to situations from our feelings, often we cause lots of problems we wouldn't have if we had been willing to do a reality check and find out what was really going on, rather than assuming we knew. It takes a lot of time and energy to undo a reaction that could have been avoided had we waited until we were sure what action was really called for here.

Let's look at an example. You're getting ready to make a big sales presentation and, like most of us, speaking in public brings up enormous anxiety. You know, the queasy stomach, the sweaty pits, the weak legs. Your mind is working overtime, worrying about being asked a question you don't know the answer to, losing your place in the presentation and skipping something important, running out of time and having to rush the grand finale that you worked so hard on. What if people act bored? What if you get a poor evaluation when it's over? Is your job in jeopardy? All of these worries cause feelings of anxiety (remember, they're not real— they're imagined).

Many people react too quickly to feelings. They assume they're real and then do one of three things:

1. Deny they are feeling anything
2. Find someone to blame for how they're feeling, and make sure they get even
3. Dump their feelings on whomever is there and manipulate them into feeling responsible for their feelings

If you've really been paying attention, you may have noticed none of those three actions work. The most dangerous of the three may actually be denial. If you refuse to know you're having feelings or an emotion, you are really leaving yourself powerless to act should the fear be real. Better to notice you're feeling afraid and then do a quick reality check with yourself: Am I in real, immediate danger here, or am I imagining a bad outcome from something that hasn't even happened yet?

If it's not real, go through this checklist, and choose some actions that will empower you.

1. Talk to a trusted friend, and get some support from a fellow salesperson.
2. If it's an important situation, get some coaching from an expert (like your sales manager).
3. Work off your anxiety with some exercise. (Do a few laps around the parking lot.)
4. Get a good night's sleep.
5. Make sure you eat a nutritious meal—coffee and sugar increase anxiety.
6. Do some deep breathing—in through the nose and out through the mouth. Make a sound as you exhale if you're really nervous (that won't be too hard). Put all of your focus on your belly as you do this.
7. A nice shower or relaxing bath does wonders for the nervous system.
8. Practice visualizing the outcome you want—getting the appointment, or making the sale, or getting a standing ovation at the end of your presentation.
9. Prayer works. Try it.

Now make a list of all your concerns (about picking up that phone and making the call or delivering a stellar presentation). Then devise a plan of action for each of them, *should they arise.* Then move forward, knowing you have done your homework and trusting that you will recognize if your fear materializes and know what to do.

Back to our example, it's important to acknowledge you're worried about that big presentation. Be very careful that you don't take your anxiety out on others in some destructive way before your presentation. Leave any other issues alone, and handle them after your presentation. Then prepare carefully, do your homework, get a good night's rest, and have a healthy meal in the morning. As you go to your presentation, do some deep breathing and keep imagining the outcome that you want from your presentation. Take these positive steps, and notice that you will be calmer and more centered during the presentation. If your fears do materialize, go into your action plan. If not, relax and enjoy. Either way, you just made fear your ally.

Now pick up the telephone, and make a sales call!

Index